CNC WOOD WORKING

FOR THE ABSOLUTE BEGINNER

CNC WOOD WORKING
FOR THE ABSOLUTE BEGINNER

WINNING TIPS, TECHNIQUES & 5 SKILL-BUILDING PROJECTS

RALPH BAGNALL

ISBN 978-1-4971-0473-0

The Cataloging-in-Publication Data is on file with the Library of Congress.

Managing Editor: Gretchen Bacon

Acquisitions Editor: Kaylee J. Schofield

Editor: Joseph Borden

Designer: Ines Freire / Alfons Freire

Proofreader: Kurt Connelly

Indexer: Jay Kreider

To learn more about the other great books from Fox Chapel Publishing,
or to find a retailer near you, call toll-free
800-457-9112, reach us by mail at 903 Square Street, Mount Joy, PA 17552, or visit us at *www. FoxChapelPublishing.com.*

We are always looking for talented authors. To submit an idea, please send a brief inquiry to acquisitions@foxchapelpublishing.com.

Printed in China
First printing

Introduction

In the decades I've been working with CNC machines, training commercial CNC operators, and teaching CNC woodworking classes for hobbyists, I've learned the fundamental questions that beginners always ask. Those questions are the reason for this book. After teaching a series of in-person classes focused on five projects, I wanted to put together a guide that helps new enthusiasts get started quickly while answering those questions to give them a good foundation. I find that students connect to the material best when it is presented in context. For example, I can explain about cutting on, inside, or outside the lines, but it makes more sense when I can show how to make these cuts in the course of making a project.

This book, like the classes, is built around five projects, each one chosen to illustrate the concepts of and techniques for programming and running your machine. The projects provide the context to help you successfully master the basic skill set of CNC woodworking. There will always be more to learn—I still learn new things with every class I teach—but this book will give you a good start.

Even an entry-level CNC machine with a small working area has amazing potential in the right hands.

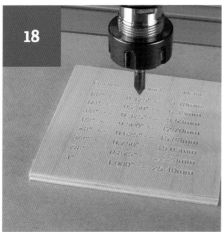

CONTENTS

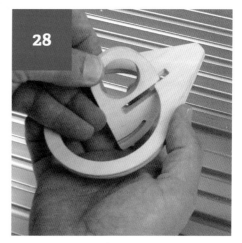

bearings, or other guides. The CNC's frame holds the router securely, and the computer's instructions tell the machine how to move the router. Servo motors move the machine's router forward, back, left, right, up, and down according to the instructions in the G-code. CNC machines can be very precise and can repeat the same movements every time the program is run, allowing you to make multiple parts that match exactly or different parts that fit together.

4. What Can a CNC Machine Make?

This fun charcuterie set was created by the author for a *Woodworker's Journal* magazine video.

Quite a lot! Without special bits or accessories, your CNC can cut different types of wood, plastic, cardboard, and phenolic. It can drill holes, mill pockets, shape and profile edges, and carve images and text. Combining these features allows you to make a wide variety of signs, plaques, tools, utensils, decorations, and models. Your imagination is the limit to what you can make.

5. How Do I Get Started?

Each of the five projects in this book are designed to walk you step by step through the basics of CNC programming and operation so you can get great results with your machine right away. When you are ready to dig deeper, my book *Complete Guide to CNC Woodworking* will teach you the more advanced lessons in programming your machine, running programs, tool choices and clamping parts for more advanced results.

Entry-Level Machines

Small CNC machines, also called benchtop CNCs, are a fairly new category of woodworking machines, and they appeal to a wide range of users who may not even think of themselves as woodworkers in the traditional sense. This growing interest in smaller machines has led to a greater range of them becoming available. They can cost anywhere from several hundred dollars to around ten thousand dollars.

A word of warning about lower-priced machines: Many brands offer models priced around $500 or less, but be careful. At this price point, they are often 12-volt DC systems, which are very low powered and will need to make many passes to cut through common materials.

Most brands have user forums you can join to get feedback and even tech support from actual users of the machines. Consider joining user forums of the brands you like before purchasing a machine, as you can get valuable information to help you decide which machine will best suit your needs.

As of this writing, the author found two "mainstream" machines for under $1,000.00 and from there you can spend up to $10,000.00. Usually, you will spend more for a bigger working envelope, but not always. A smaller machine with a robust frame may cost more than a lighter weight machine with a larger working envelope.

Eye, hearing, and lung protection are essential to any woodworking project.

As I mentioned, over many years in CNC woodworking, I've identified the most common questions asked by beginners. So let's start by looking at these five questions and their answers before moving on to the projects.

Five Common Questions

1. What Is a CNC Machine?

A CNC machine for wood can be thought of as simply a router that is guided by motors and a frame, based on instructions from a computer, rather than by your hands. CNC is an abbreviation for **computer numerical control**, meaning that a computer program you create tells the machine how to move and what cuts to make. A CNC machine can make the same cuts as a hand router but with greater accuracy.

While CNC machines can look very different, most share the same basic components shown in the illustration. The router bit, which does the cutting, is secured in the router motor, or spindle. The router is held in a bracket that moves up and down in the Z-axis and is powered by a servo motor. The router and Z-axis servo motor move side to side in the X-axis along the bridge, and the entire bridge moves in the Y-axis, going forward and backward over the workpiece, or part, which is secured onto the bed. Servo motors on all three axes move the router bit very precisely, allowing the part to be cut in three dimensions.

2. Do I Need to Be a Computer Expert?

No. I have always found it easier to teach a woodworker how to program a CNC machine than to teach a programmer how to work in wood. If you are already a woodworker, your experience with routers, bits, grain direction, and milling wood will be directly relevant to programming the CNC.

The software used to program CNC machines is called CAD/CAM software (CAD stands for computer-aided design, and CAM stands for computer-aided manufacturing). It will do most of the work for you in telling the router what to do.

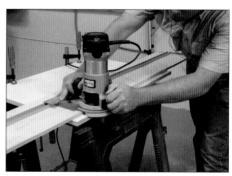

Your woodworking experience using hand routers and other tools will help when learning to program the CNC.

You will draw out all the details of the project and assign the cuts that the machine will make. You will send all this information to the machine in a programming language called **G-code**. The G-code file turns the machine on, runs the tasks contained in the program, and stops the process when it is complete.

We will import some ready-to-use drawings, and we will create other drawings in the CAD side of the software. Then the lines, holes, and text in the drawing will be assigned a router bit we want to use, how deep to cut, and at what speed. This is the CAM part of the software.

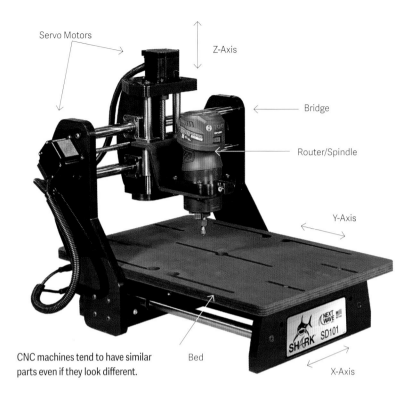

Servo Motors

Z-Axis

Bridge

Router/Spindle

Y-Axis

X-Axis

Bed

CNC machines tend to have similar parts even if they look different.

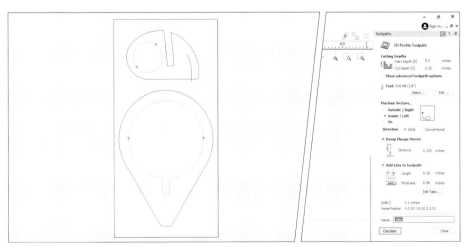

The software prompts you for the information it needs, shortening your learning curve.

You will do most of this programming by working through a list of options on the screen and entering the data you want to use. If you can open programs, find files, import files, and perform basic mouse functions, you will be able to use CAD/CAM software packages. Like I said, it really is easier for a woodworker to learn the software than for a software engineer to learn how to work in wood!

3. How Does a CNC Machine Work?
A CNC machine works very much like a hand router, but it does not need templates,

bearings, or other guides. The CNC's frame holds the router securely, and the computer's instructions tell the machine how to move the router. Servo motors move the machine's router forward, back, left, right, up, and down according to the instructions in the G-code. CNC machines can be very precise and can repeat the same movements every time the program is run, allowing you to make multiple parts that match exactly or different parts that fit together.

4. What Can a CNC Machine Make?

This fun charcuterie set was created by the author for a *Woodworker's Journal* magazine video.

Quite a lot! Without special bits or accessories, your CNC can cut different types of wood, plastic, cardboard, and phenolic. It can drill holes, mill pockets, shape and profile edges, and carve images and text. Combining these features allows you to make a wide variety of signs, plaques, tools, utensils, decorations, and models. Your imagination is the limit to what you can make.

5. How Do I Get Started?

Each of the five projects in this book are designed to walk you step by step through the basics of CNC programming and operation so you can get great results with your machine right away. When you are ready to dig deeper, my book *Complete Guide to CNC Woodworking* will teach you the more advanced lessons in programming your machine, running programs, tool choices and clamping parts for more advanced results.

Entry-Level Machines

Small CNC machines, also called benchtop CNCs, are a fairly new category of woodworking machines, and they appeal to a wide range of users who may not even think of themselves as woodworkers in the traditional sense. This growing interest in smaller machines has led to a greater range of them becoming available. They can cost anywhere from several hundred dollars to around ten thousand dollars.

A word of warning about lower-priced machines: Many brands offer models priced around $500 or less, but be careful. At this price point, they are often 12-volt DC systems, which are very low powered and will need to make many passes to cut through common materials.

Most brands have user forums you can join to get feedback and even tech support from actual users of the machines. Consider joining user forums of the brands you like before purchasing a machine, as you can get valuable information to help you decide which machine will best suit your needs.

As of this writing, the author found two "mainstream" machines for under $1,000.00 and from there you can spend up to $10,000.00. Usually, you will spend more for a bigger working envelope, but not always. A smaller machine with a robust frame may cost more than a lighter weight machine with a larger working envelope.

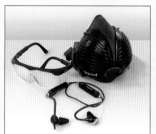

Eye, hearing, and lung protection are essential to any woodworking project.

Here are a few examples of benchtop CNCs for you to consider. There are many more out there, and this list is not a recommendation from the author. It is just a look at some of the many options available.

Photo courtesy of Stepcraft USA

Stepcraft's D420 machine has an 11.7" (300mm) x 16.3" (415mm) bed.

This ShopBot Desktop 1824 is the one the author used in this boo.

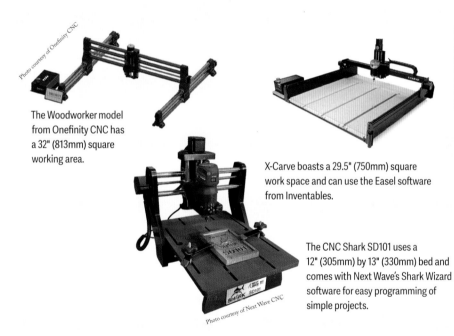

Photo courtesy of Onefinity CNC

The Woodworker model from Onefinity CNC has a 32" (813mm) square working area.

Photo courtesy of Inventables, Inc.

X-Carve boasts a 29.5" (750mm) square work space and can use the Easel software from Inventables.

The CNC Shark SD101 uses a 12" (305mm) by 13" (330mm) bed and comes with Next Wave's Shark Wizard software for easy programming of simple projects.

Photo courtesy of Next Wave CNC

Shop Safety

Your CNC machine moves itself automatically once you initiate a program, but as with any power tool, you should use standard safety equipment. When cutting, a CNC is just as loud as a handheld router. Wear hearing protection when the machine is running. Safety glasses are also a must. Chips and even cut parts can be ejected from the work area, so protecting your eyes is important. Wood dust, especially from exotic woods, can cause irritation and even allergic reactions in some people. A dust mask or a good respirator will help keep your lungs clean and healthy. Use your common sense and remember that you are your own best protection.

Choosing Bits for Your CNC Machine

A wide range of router bits are now made specifically for use in benchtop CNCs, but most of your "standard" router bits can be used as well.

New CNC users often ask which bits can be used with their machines. The short answer is that you can, in most cases, use the same bits as you would with your handheld router and router table. Excepting bearing-guided router bits, the line between CNC bits and router bits is nearly nonexistent now.

While there are specialty bits in the industrial market made specifically for CNC use, these are generally designed to perform at feeds and speeds far faster than any benchtop machines are capable of, so they are unsuitable for benchtop machines. Spiral bits are an exception; having initially been designed for CNC use, they have become popular for handheld routers as well.

I mentioned that you cannot use bearing-guided bits with your CNC machine. In your handheld router, the bearing rides along the edge of the part, with your arms acting as "springs" to control the contact and follow the edge. On your CNC, you do not need to use the bearing for control, and the machine frame controls where the bit goes, so a bearing will simply get in the way. There remain many styles and types of bits you can use with your CNC.

You also must consider the size of your bits. For example, my CNC Shark uses a Bosch Colt router for the motor, So I use ¼" (8mm) shank bits with it. My ShopBot has a spindle that can take any shank size up to ½" (12mm).

A selection of router bits that I have used with both my handheld router and CNC machine.

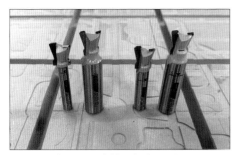

Most router bits are available in both ½" (12mm) and ¼" (6mm) shank sizes. This dovetail bit from MicroJig is also available with 8mm and 12mm shanks to fit European routers.

Router bits usually consist of a steel shank and body with carbide tips brazed onto it, but bits also can be milled from solid carbide. These two straight bits are made differently but make the same cut in your CNC.

If your system can use ½" (12mm) shank bits, you should use them whenever possible. A ½" (12mm) shank bit is not twice as stiff as a ¼" (6mm) shank; it is actually eight times stiffer, which means much less vibration and cleaner cuts at higher feed rates. The only exception to this rule of thumb is when using a ¼"-diameter or smaller bit. To make a ¼" (6mm) -diameter bit with a ½" (12mm) shank, the body must be turned down on a lathe, and the neck where this transition is made is always the weak part. I have broken a number of ¼" (6mm) bits with ½" (12mm) shanks, but very few ¼" (6mm) bits with ¼" (6mm) shanks. Those using metric bits will generally need to choose between 8mm and 12mm shank bits. The same rules apply, so use the bigger shank where possible.

Carbide Tip and Solid Carbide

Many bits are made as a steel body with carbide cutting edges braised on, and others are milled completely from a single piece of solid carbide. In many cases, the same size/type of bit are available in both configurations. There are technical differences, but at the feeds and speeds at which our benchtop CNCs are operating, there is no specific benefit to either type. You can find many ¼" (6mm) and ½" (12mm) straight bits, V bits, and fluting bits in steel body or solid carbide. However, the ⅛" (3mm) and ¹⁄₁₆" (2mm) bits we'll be using later in the book are solid carbide because it is more difficult to braise such thin carbide pieces to a steel shank.

Steel-body bits tend to be a bit less expensive. Buy what's available in the size, shape, and price that work for you.

Spiral Bits

Spiral bits are good general-purpose bits, and they can cut at higher feed speeds than an equivalent straight bit. With many materials, they provide a smooth cut. The curve of the spiral bit's cutting edge has the same effect as angling a hand plane or chisel during a cut; the angle creates a shearing cut like a knife rather than a straight, chopping cut like a chisel. This can be a great advantage allowing for higher feed speeds with lower RPM to avoid friction and heat.

Spiral bits aren't always the best choice, though. They cut plywood quickly, but the edge of the cut will be much less smooth than a cut made with a simple steel-body straight bit with carbide cutters. Spiral bits tend to perform better when cutting with the grain

While one of these bits is spiral ground and the other is not, both make the same flat-walled, flat-bottomed cut when mounted in your CNC. In plywood, the straight bit on the right typically makes a better cut.

than when cutting against it, so plywood edges cut with spiral bits tend to be fuzzy between layers where the grain direction changes. When cutting plywood, the slower-cutting straight bit will save you time because the edges of the parts won't need as much sanding after milling.

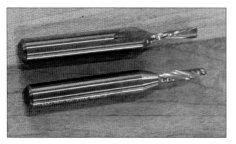

An upshear spiral cutting edge twists up from tip to shank, while the downshear twists down from shank to tip. Even though both make the same size cut, the upshear removes chips better from deep grooves and pockets while the downshear provides chip free cutting with veneers and laminates.

Spiral bits are made in both "up" and "down" configurations. The up or down is based on the direction of the spiral twist relative to the tip. An up spiral bit will pull chips up out of the kerf being cut, much like a drill bit. A down spiral bit pushes the chips toward the stock being cut. The lifting cut of the up spiral helps clear chips in deep slots, but it also tends to tear out the fragile face veneer layer on plywood. When I'm cutting shallow pockets and dadoes in plywood, I use a down spiral. The spiral cuts down into the panel from above, so the fragile veneer layer is supported by the substrate as it is cut, leaving the top edges clean and smooth.

Machinists' End Mills

Many CAD/CAM programs refer to straight bits as "end mills." This is a holdover from the metal machining industry, where CNCs got their start. While typical woodworking bits are technically end mills, they are not interchangeable with end mills made for cutting metals. The feeds and speeds needed for woodworking are simply not compatible with metal cutting tools, so stick to woodworking bits in your CNC.

The many cutting edges of the end mill shown here work well with metals, but in wood the extra cutting edges generate excessive friction. Benchtop CNCs work better with one- or two-flute bits than end mills.

Profile Bits

Most profile router bits are bearing guided and unsuitable for CNC use, but you can still find a wide range without bearings. These can greatly expand your CNC machine's capabilities. V bits, dovetail bits, roundovers, and ogee bits are just a few of the profiles available. Using these alongside your straight bits allows for carving text and images into a sign, adding a nice profile to the edge, and cutting it out all on the CNC. Creative use of profile bits with your machine will take your projects to another level.

There are there are many discount bits on the market, but you are not saving money if the cut quality is poor or if you have to replace your bits more often. The reputable brands you prefer for your handheld router bits should be your go-to sources for CNC bits as well.

Many manufacturers are now offering sets of bits for CNC users. I have always advised caution when buying bit sets for handheld routers, and the same goes for these CNC kits. A set that includes a couple straight cutters in

Both of these bits cut the same profile, but only bits without pilot bearings can be used in your CNC machine.

A surprising number of the router bits in a woodworking collection can be used in a benchtop CNC machine as well.

common sizes, V bits in 90 and 60 degrees, and a round nose or two is a good place to start, but a set of ten or more bits usually means that a few get used regularly, and a bunch more just gather dust. I generally prefer to buy bits as I need them. It seems to save money over the long term.

The bottom line is that using a clean, sharp bit at the proper feed rate and RPM will provide the best results on your CNC just as it will with your handheld or table router. I keep all my router bits in one dedicated cabinet and often use the same bits for handheld routing and CNC work.

Bit and Collet Maintenance

A little-known fact among woodworkers is that carbide bits and blades are rarely worn out through use. What we call "getting dull" is most often the carbide being damaged by heat. Carbide is not a solid metal like steel; it is made up of carbide particles bonded together with another metal, often tungsten. Excessive heating of the carbide tips causes the binder to break down, releasing the carbide particles. This happens first at the cutting edge, where the carbide is thinnest and heats fastest.

Your bits and collets require regular cleaning and maintenance just as your CNC machine does to provide you with the best possible performance.

The bit on the right has been damaged through excessive heat during cutting. It is beyond repair and should be recycled.

When a bit is cutting, the heat that develops tends to vaporize the sap or resins in solid woods and the glues in sheet goods. This vapor will condense onto the first cooler surface it touches, which will usually be the back bevels of the carbide, the bit shank, and the collet. This is the "gunk" that you see appearing on your bits and blades when you are using any tool. As these burned-on deposits build up behind the cutting edges, they start to rub against the stock being cut and add to the friction heat that is damaging your bits and reducing their cutting performance. So keeping bits clean is crucial.

Many commercial cleaners are formulated specifically for woodworking bits and blades, and, fortunately, many are made from organic and noncaustic bases, so they are much safer to use in the home shop. Some formulas use citric acid from oranges and lemons to clean, and I have had great success with soy-based products as well. Regardless of what cleaning product you choose, clean your tooling regularly.

I often start by removing the bulk of the buildup with a razor blade, then I soak the bits in the cleaner. You can scrub your bits

Cleaning some bits. Cleaning stations like this one from MicroJig can help you spend less time cleaning and more time cutting.

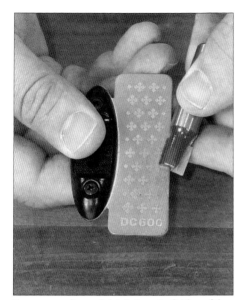

You can use a diamond plate to hone the flat face of the carbide cutters on your bits. This can refresh the edge and extend the bit life.

Collets are not designed to last forever and should be replaced every two to three years depending on how often you use your CNC.

with a brass wire brush, steel wool, or even nonwoven abrasives like Scotch-Brite™. Don't forget to inspect and clean your collets, too. If there is buildup on the shanks of your bits, then the collet also will be dirty. Dirty collets can lead to excess vibration of the bit and can even cause the bit to slip out of the collet, potentially damaging parts and your machine.

Testing the sharpness of a router bit by feeling the edge with your finger or thumb is simply not a reliable gauge. "Sharpness" is about not only the cutting edge but also the clearance bevels of the blades, and those are much more difficult to test. If your bit is clean and cuts poorly or makes excessive noise when cutting (compared to a newer bit), then it has likely come to the end of its useful life span and needs to be replaced. Except for physical damage to the carbide or overheating, you can expect to get many hours of actual cutting time from your bits on the CNC.

If the bit has not been burned nor the cutting edge chipped, honing the face of a bit can refresh the edge and extend the life of the bit. A diamond sharpening stone

or card (see photo above, left) works quite well on carbide. Just hold the bit with the carbide face flat to the stone and rub it back and forth, keeping the face firmly pressed against the stone. Do not try to sharpen the carbide's beveled edge or change the shape of its straight or curved profile in the process. You want to hone only the flat face of the carbide. This may seem counterintuitive, but by flattening the face, you restore the cutting edge with little or no change to the bit diameter or profile shape.

One final note here: router collets do not last forever. The inner sleeve inside the nut that holds the bit (see photo above, right) is made of spring steel so that it can compress to clamp your bit in place. The heating and cooling it experiences with each use eventually reverses the heat treatment it got during manufacturing to make it flexible.

With daily use, router collets (CNC or handheld) should be replaced every year. In home shop use, consider replacing collets every two or three years, depending on how often you use them. The recommendation from collet manufacturers is to replace them after around 500 hours of use.

CHAPTER 1

CONVERSION CHART COASTER

This is a simple project designed to guide you through the mechanics of your first CNC project. You will engrave a conversion chart onto a small part with no holes or cutting through. The aim of the project is to walk you step by step through setting up and running your machine. The other projects in the book will teach you specific skills, but this one will be easy and will guide you through importing a file, using your software, setting up your machine, and running your first program.

For these projects, I used VCarve Pro because it is the most common CNC program in use today. Do not worry if you are using another program; the steps and even the icons should be similar between programs. Also, I used a ShopBot Desktop CNC and an Axiom CNC so you can see how they differ but also how they work in much the same way as each other. Your machine will likely be similar to these models.

Supplies

- 4" (100mm) x 4" (100mm) x ¼" (6mm) good-quality plywood
- 60-degree V bit (Whiteside 1541 or similar)

Skill Building

In this project, you will:
- Set up a new job.
- Import a file.
- Create a text toolpath.
- Output G-code for the machine.
- Prepare the CNC to cut.
- Run your first project.

X, Y, and Z Axes

Your CNC is a three-axis machine, with one axis for each dimension: length, width, and height. These are often referred to as Cartesian coordinates, and CNC machines identify them as the X-axis, the Y-axis, and the Z-axis, respectively. Generally, the X-axis is the left-to-right dimension across the bed of your machine, and the Y-axis is measured front to back along the bed. The Z-axis is always oriented up and down and controls the bit height when cutting the project. Note the X, Y, and Z icons at the top of the workspace in the figure to the right. The axes are usually labeled on the machine itself, but be sure to check yours, as some machines reverse the X- and Y-axes.

Your first complete CNC project.

Fraction		Decimal		Metric
1/8"	⬦	0.125"	⬦	3.18mm
1/4"	⬦	0.250"	⬦	6.35mm
3/8"	⬦	0.375"	⬦	9.53mm
1/2"	⬦	0.500"	⬦	12.70mm
5/8"	⬦	0.625"	⬦	15.88mm
3/4"	⬦	0.750"	⬦	19.05mm
7/8"	⬦	0.875"	⬦	22.23mm
1"	⬦	1.000"	⬦	25.40mm

Download the companion files
for this project by scanning
the QR code above or visiting
www.foxpatterns.com/
cnc-woodworking-for-the-
absolute-beginner.

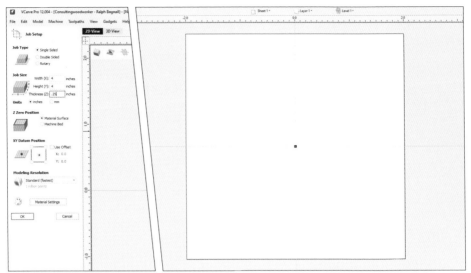

1 **Set up the size of the job.** Open the CAD/CAM software and select the Create New File or Create New Job option. A Job Setup dialog box will open, providing a list of settings for you to select for your project. This project will be single sided and will use a 4" square stock or workpiece. Enter 4" (100mm) for both the X-axis and the Y-axis. The software works equally well in inches or millimeters. Type in the thickness of your stock in the box provided. The stock shown is 0.25" (6mm) thick. Check the box to set the Z-zero position to Material Surface so the program starts at the top of your part and works down. There are special cases where Machine Bed is the zero position, but this is rare. The XY Datum Position box shows a workspace, and this is where you tell the computer where on the part to start the program. You can select one of the four corners or the center. Most often, the lower left corner or the center of the stock is used. Select the center point for this program. Uncheck the Use Offset box if it is selected so your program will start at the center as selected. Once you have entered these choices for your project, click on OK to open to the work area of the program. (Note: You'll see that a couple of advanced options are available under Modeling Resolution, but you should leave them at the default settings.)

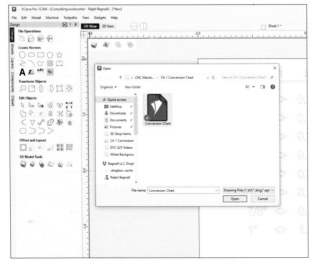

2 **Import a premade file into your CAD/CAM software.** To do this, select File > Import > Import Vectors, or Click on the Import Vectors icon in the top row on the left of your screen. Use the browser window that opens to select the Conversion Chart.dxf file from the companion programs for this book, downloaded via the QR code provided at the start of this chapter.

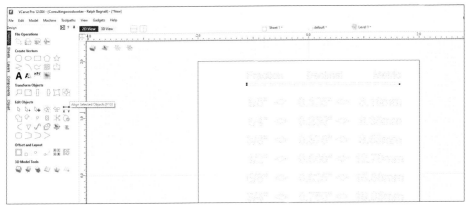

3 **Align the imported items on the workspace.** The imported file will appear on the screen but may not be located where you want in the work zone. This is the "offset" we chose not to use when setting up the job, and it is easy to fix. The imported chart will appear as red dashed lines, meaning it is already selected. If it is not, just use your mouse to click and drag over the entire image to select it. Click on the Align Selected Objects icon to open the Alignment Tools dialog box. Then click on the center icon in the Align to Material section at the top, which will center the chart on your workspace.

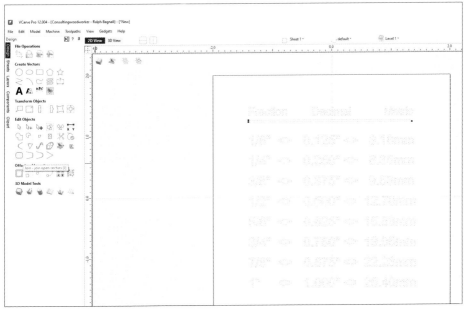

4 **Select the entire import and click on Join Open Vectors.** These **.dxf files** are made up of many individual lines and arcs that you see as a single item, but the computer sees unrelated lines and curves. With all imported files, you will combine these lines and curves into sets so the machine can work with them. Do this using the Join Open Vectors command. When the dialog box opens, select the entire chart if it is not already red. In the dialog box, make sure the tolerance is set to 0.03" (0.7mm), click on the Join button, and close the dialog box.

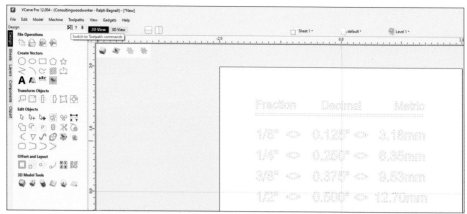

5 **Open the toolpaths.** In most CAD/CAM programs, there are different areas for the setup and drawing tasks we have been using so far, and a section used for telling the CNC machine what to cut and how. In VCarve, click on Toolpaths on the top menu bar to access the Toolpath commands and begin the next part of this project. This is the CAM (computer-aided manufacturing) part of the CAD/CAM program, where actual tools and cuts are applied to the drawing. Select all the text you just imported, then click on the VCarve/Engraving Toolpath icon in the menu box on the right. This will open a dialog box where you can fill in the data needed. These toolpath dialog boxes are designed to make it easy for you to program your CNC by just filling in the data boxes in sequence.

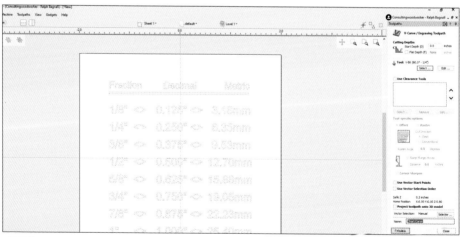

6 **Select your tools and calculate the toolpath.** The first box is Cutting Depths. With engraving, which is also called V-carving, you do not enter a depth because the size and shape of the letters and numbers being carved determine the cut depth, so you can move on to the next box. We will cover engraving in detail in Chapter 4. Choose the tool (router bit) in the next box. Click on the Select box and a Tool Database will pop up with a list of router bits for you to choose from. In this case, we want to use a 60-degree V bit. Select it from the database and click Select to return to the Engraving Toolpath box. The only other decision to make here is to name the toolpath. There is only one toolpath in this program, but now is the time to start building good habits by always naming your individual toolpaths. Being able to find particular steps will save you time as your programs get more complicated and you need to edit them. Name this toolpath Chart Carve and click the Calculate button at the bottom.

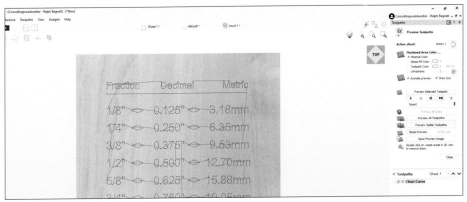

7 **Review your calculated toolpath for any errors.** The toolpath you just calculated is now shown as a 3D model in the main work area. You'll notice that there are red and blue lines that do not quite look like a carved part. The blue lines show where the center of the router bit will cut, and the red lines represent the rapid travel movements that the head of the CNC machine makes between cuts. The right-hand dialog box has also changed and is now showing the Preview Toolpaths options. Click on the Preview Selected Toolpath button at the top. The colored lines will vanish, and you will see an accurate representation of the carving as it will be made by your CNC.

Tool Database

The router bits you will be using with your CNC will be recorded in your **Tool Database**. The database lets you name the tool and define it by diameter, shape, depth of cut, **feed speed**, and other parameters. Most CAD/CAM programs come with some common tools preloaded, and over time you can add the new ones that you use. The database lets you set the feeds and speeds that you prefer for your machine as defaults, so you won't need to specify these settings with every toolpath you program. When needed, you can edit the defaults when setting up a particular toolpath without altering the database settings.

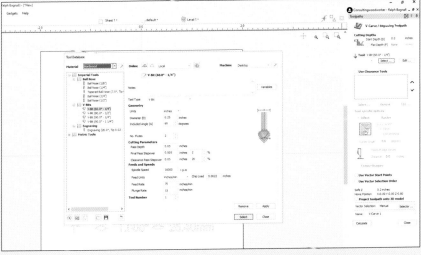

You can add, select, and change parameters for your router bits (tools) in the Tool Database.

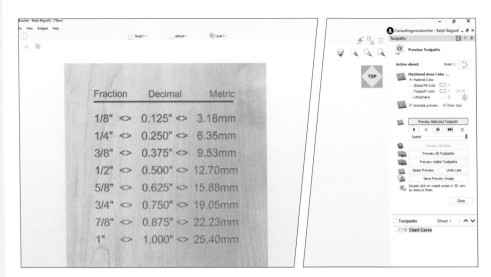

8 **Convert all the CAD/CAM information into G-code.** The computer that drives the CNC is not very sophisticated; it can only read a text file that tells it where to move step by step using a file called a G-code. The final step before turning on your CNC machine is to convert all the CAD/CAM information you selected into the G-code that your CNC can follow.

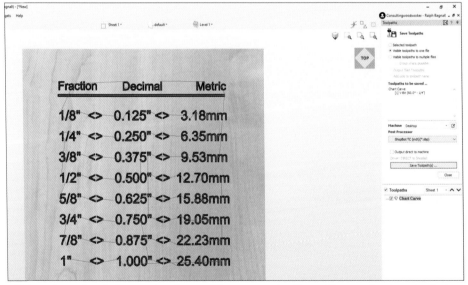

9 **Save the toolpath.** Ensure that the small box next to the Carve Chart toolpath is checked, then close the Preview Toolpaths dialog box and click on the Save Toolpath icon at the bottom right to open up a new dialog box. You will need to select the post processor for your machine. Your machine's manual should tell you which post processor to select. In this case, I have selected the post processor for my ShopBot Desktop CNC. Click on Save Toolpath and save the file with an appropriate name. While you are at it, be sure to save the VCarve program with a similar name so you know the two are related.

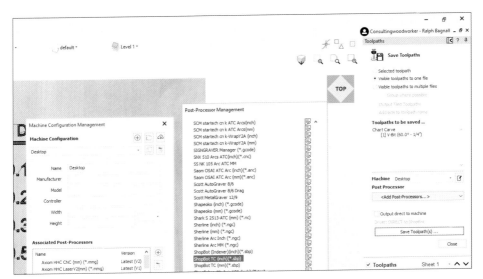

10 **Select the post processor.** Once you select the post processor the first time, you should never need to change it unless you get a different CNC.

One Program for One Project

Do not get confused about the various programs we are discussing here. You only need to work with the CAD/CAM program, which is VCarve in this case. VCarve is where we put in the drawings and then instruct the machine how and where to cut. The post processor takes all that information and converts it into a simple text file that the machine understands. You only need to choose the post processor the first time you output a program unless you change machines. The text file that the machine runs on is called a G-code. You need to save the G-code from VCarve, then select it to to run your CNC. You don't need to open or work within either the post processor or the G-Code files.

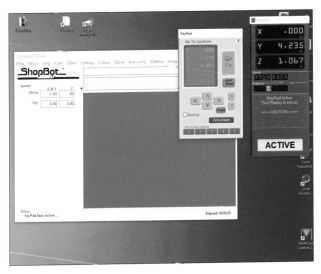

11 **Follow your machine's instructions to plug it in, turn the system on, and connect it to your computer if needed.** Some machines are controlled from the screen of your computer; others are controlled from a pendant attached to the machine and do not need to be connected to a computer. Most machines need to be homed so the system knows where the head is located. Follow the instructions to home your CNC and get it ready to begin operations.

12 Secure the 60-degree V bit into the collet of your CNC. You should secure it in the same way you would for a hand router. The bit should fill at least two-thirds of the collet, but with the cutting edges fully exposed. Tighten the collet nut to secure the bit as shown in the image accompanying this step. Some routers will use two wrenches, while others will use a single wrench and a spindle lock button built into the router.

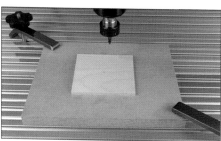

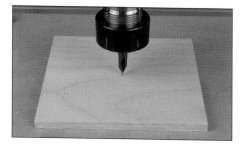

13 Jog the head back to access the machine bed and secure the workpiece in place. Because this chart is a small part that will be carved over most of its face, use double-sided tape to secure it to a larger piece of scrap wood. This larger part allows the clamps to hold the work without being in the toolpath. Place the part on the machine bed and secure it using the clamps that came with your machine as shown above. The exact position is not important; just set the workpiece so it is square to the bed. Make a small pencil mark at the center of the 4" square blank; this will be the Zero or start point for the program. Following your machine's instructions, Raise the Z-axis so the head is clear of the part and clamps, then jog the head in the X- and Y-axes to position it over the workpiece. Lower the Z-axis until the tip of the bit is just above the workpiece. Your CNC controller software or pendant has a Step feature to move the head in very small increments for precise positioning. Using the bit as a pointer, slowly move the head in X- and Y-axes until the tip is centered on the pencil mark. Reset the X- and Y-axes to zero as described in your CNC machine's manual.

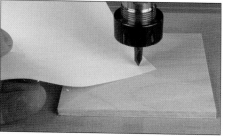

14 Set the Z-axis. The CNC now knows where to start the program in X and Y, but not in Z, so you need to set the point where the bit meets the top of the stock. Many machines have a touch plate system to automatically set the Z-axis to zero. If your machine has this feature, use it by following your machine's instruction manual; otherwise, set the Z-zero manually according to the following steps: Hold a piece of lightweight paper on top of the stock and step the Z-axis down toward the part. Slide the paper back and forth under the bit as you lower it until you feel the paper dragging under the tip of the bit. Set the Z-axis to zero at this point, then jog the Z-axis up off the stock. You are ready to run your first program.

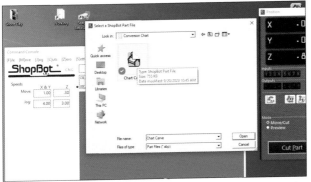 

15 **Begin running your CNC program.** To begin cutting, select the G-code program file, Chart Carve, that you saved earlier. The exact process for telling the program to run will vary from machine to machine, and your manual will have the details for your CNC. If you need to manually start your router, turn it on now. The bit should be set to around 16,000 RPM. If you've set everything up correctly, your CNC machine should begin engraving the conversion chart into your stock. All cutting should happen within the 4" square, and the cuts should be quite shallow. So, as the router begins to move, watch carefully and be ready to hit the Pause or Stop button if the bit travels outside the work area or starts cutting deep into the part. With my machine, the program takes about eight minutes to run; there is a lot of detail in this design.

16 **Finish the program and remove workpiece from machine.** Once the program finishes, the router will rise up, away from the stock, and either stop where it is or return to the X, Y-zero location where it started. You have successfully run your first CNC program on your new machine! Shut the router motor off if needed and jog the head back to give you access to remove the workpiece from the machine.

17 **Finish your workpiece.** Depending on your stock, the engraving may be clear and visible, or it may not be. You can enhance it by painting the stock and sanding the face, leaving the paint only in the engraved areas. You can also try painting the part before milling so the engraving cuts through the paint. Your CNC gives you many options for creating wonderful things.

CHAPTER 2

DRINK HOLDER

This packable cup holder is perfect for holding hot drinks from the hotel lobby or coffee shop when you are away from home. It is easy and inexpensive to make and can be personalized as a gift. I created this design specifically to introduce you to the Profile Toolpath commands within your CAD/CAM software and to show you how they work and when to use them.

Supplies

- 4" (100mm) x 8" (200mm) x ¼" (6mm) good-quality plywood
- ⅛" (3mm) diameter straight bit (SpeTool W04006 or similar)

Skill Building

In this project, you will:
- Group objects.
- Program profile toolpaths.
- Set up cuts that are centered on lines.
- Create tabs for holding parts.
- Cut parts inside and outside of lines.

1 **Select and open the existing job file.** Select the Open an Existing File command and choose the Coffee Holder.dxf file from the download file set (accessed via the QR code on page 29) for download. Selecting the .dxf file works the same as opening a VCarve saved file: the screen will open to the Job Setup dialog box. Note that the X and Y dimensions for Job Size are automatically filled in to fit the .dxf file parameters exactly. Because a .dxf file has no Z-axis, the thickness will remain the same as what you entered for the previous job. For this file, the job size opens as 3.625" (92.07mm) for the X-axis and 7.195" (182.75mm) for the Y-axis.

This clever hot drink holder will introduce you to cutting parts using the Profile Toolpath commands.

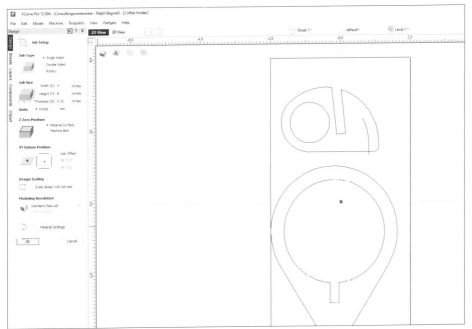

2 **Set up the job size.** The preview function works best when the virtual stock is the same size as your actual part, because what you see on the screen now will be the same on the machine later. Enter 4" (100mm) as the width (X-axis) of the stock, 8" (200mm) as the height (Y-axis), and 0.25" (6mm) as the thickness in the Z-axis. This will allow you to see all the cuts, including any tabs that may not show in the preview if the job size is exactly the size of the .dxf file. Select the center of the workpiece for the XY datum position, then uncheck the Use Offset box just as you did in Chapter 1.

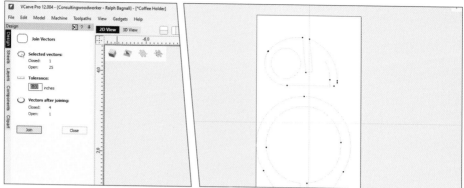

3 **Select the entire imported drawing and join the vectors.** After selecting the drawing, click on the Join Vectors icon. Note at the top of the dialog box that while this drawing looks complete, there is only one closed vector: the circle inside the upper part. The computer sees the rest as twenty-five individual, or open, vectors. Typically, these are meant to be connected to the closed-vector single objects your eye sees. This Join Vectors command lets you tell the software to join up and connect the ends of any two parts that are within the number entered in the Tolerance box. Most of these ends are already very close, but the computer will not connect them without instruction. Set the tolerance to 0.03" (0.7mm) and check the results. The Vectors after joining are shown below the Tolerance box and should indicate 4 closed vectors and 1 open vector. The closed vectors are the main bodies, and the open vector is the curved line in the top part. You can increase the tolerance to repair bigger issues, but only up to a point. A bad drawing may need to be reworked.

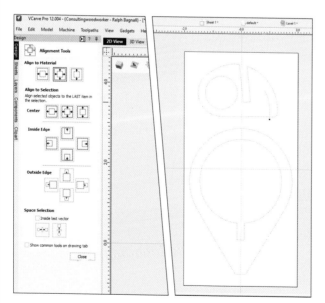

4 **Select and align your drawing objects.** The parts on your screen are in the corner of the virtual stock, but you want them centered. Select all the items, then center them by clicking on the Align Selected Object icon under the Transform Objects heading. The extra space we added to the job size allows for placing clamps in the corners of the stock, well away from the toolpath. You need this room so the bit does not hit any clamps and also so you have clearance for the collet nut and any dust shroud you may be using. At the top of this dialog box, select the center button under the Align to Material heading. This will automatically center all the selected parts side to side and top to bottom on your workpiece.

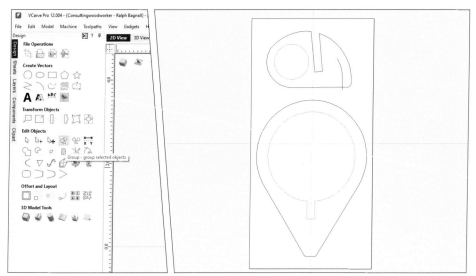

5 **Group the objects, if needed.** For multiple objects that will be milled in the same way, you can make then into a group that is selected or deselected all together. All objects in a group will be cut using the same toolpath data, so only group objects that have the same toolpath and depth. In the photo above, the inner openings of the two parts will be cut to the same depth, with the same bit, and to the inside of the lines, so they are grouped together. Note that the lines of selected objects change from red dotted lines to solid red lines when added to a group. Now select the outer lines of both parts and create a second group. Open vectors can be grouped, as you will see in Chapter 3, but because we only have one line here, and it will be cut differently than the others, it is not grouped. Now the drawing is fully prepared, and you can begin creating the toolpaths by clicking on Toolpaths at the top of the page as we did in Chapter 1. The Toolpath commands menu opens on the right side of your screen, indicating that you have switched from the CAD (drawing) part of the job to the part where you choose how to make the actual cuts, the CAM (manufacturing) part of your software.

6 **Create the Profile Toolpath.** This project is all about the Profile Toolpath. In the CNC world, Profile refers to vectors being cut on or alongside the lines. This is the most common type of toolpath, and it is calculated by the computer differently than the other toolpath types we will be using in later chapters. Select the single curved vector that creates the spring of the drink holder, then click on the Profile Toolpath icon at the top left of the menu box (pictured to the left). This toolpath will apply only to the selected vectors when you calculate the toolpath. The 2D Profile Toolpath dialog box will open with prompts for you to fill in. Just work from the top down, filling in the data as required.

Avoiding Clamps

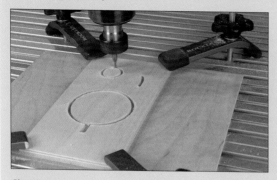

Clamps need to be kept outside the areas where the bit will be cutting.

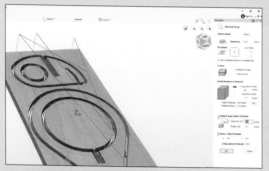

You have the option in the program to raise the bit above any obstructions, which will help you avoid clamps.

The stock size for the drink holder is large enough to provide space for the clamps around the edges to be out of the cutting path. As one cut finishes, the bit rises above the material and moves to the next cut. To save time, the Z-clearance for this defaults to about 0.2" (5mm) in most software packages. You know where the machine will move to make cuts, but where the path goes between cuts is not always clear. These rapid travel moves from the end of one cut to the start of the next show up as red lines in VCarve, but any clamps or hold-downs being used are not shown.

You can choose the height you want for this Z-clearance. You can make it smaller when carving a lot of text to minimize the up-and-down movements, but any time you are worried about your bit possibly hitting a clamp, you should set the Z-clearance higher. All CAD/CAM programs have this setting; in VCarve, it is above where you choose your toolpath under Material Setup. Just remember that it will typically stay at whatever you set it to until you change it again.

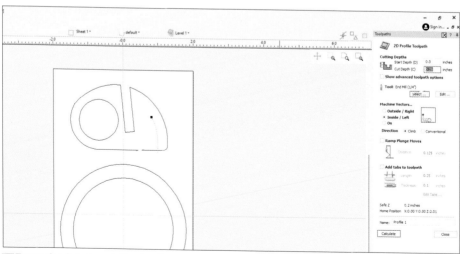

7 Enter the data to cut the depth. The first entry is for the depth of the cut. This is where the 2D drawing starts to become a 3D part. Fill in 0.00 for Start Depth, so the cut starts at the top of the material. You want to cut this slot all the way through the plywood, so specify 0.25" (6mm) for Cut Depth.

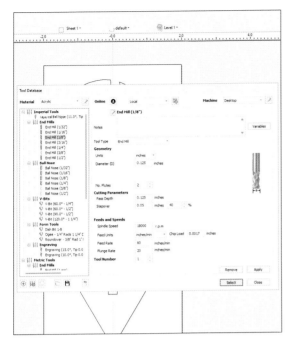

8 **Select the bits.** Working down, select the bit you want to use. This design is created for a ⅛" (3mm) straight bit. Click on the Select button to open the Tool Database and choose the ⅛" (3mm) tool. You can add this tool if needed, but most CAD/CAM programs come with a basic set of tools already in the database. Check the feed rate and plunge rate for your bit, especially the first time you select it. Most benchtop machines will feed this sort of bit between 40" and 70" per minute, depending on how ridged the machine frame is. Enter a lower number at first, then increase the feed rate gradually as you get to know your machine. Click Select to use the ⅛" (3mm) bit after you've adjusted the parameters, if needed.

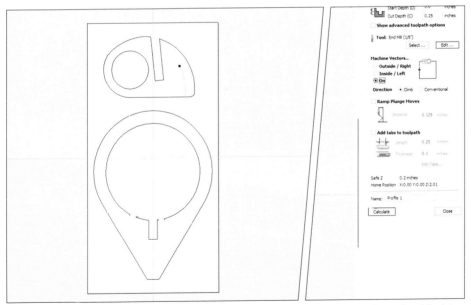

9 **Align the tool to the lines being cut.** The next box down, after selecting the tool, is Machine Vectors, where you choose how the tool will align to the lines being cut. In this case, you want to cut **on** the line, meaning that the center of the bit follows the center of the line, so select the On option. Note that there is a small drawing to the right of the Machine Vectors box that shows which condition you selected and how the bit will travel. Finally, you can select the direction to climb-cut or conventionally cut the part. While we generally avoid climb-cutting with handhold and table routers, the CNC machine has no issues with climb-cutting; in fact, it is preferred for cleaner cuts with loss tear-out in solid wood stock.

10 **Use ramps to protect your router bits.** The box under Machine Vectors is Ramp Plunge Moves. Understanding and using the ramp will greatly improve the life of your router bits. Plunging or drilling straight down into the stock with a bit turning at high speed will create a lot of friction, which becomes heat. This heat can burn your wood and damage the carbide in the bit. Even coated bits will be damaged prematurely if exposed to excess heat. Using the Ramp command, the software will automatically move the bit side to side along the toolpath as it moves down in the Z-axis to the cut depth. The program will also add the moves needed to remove the ramp at the end of the cut, so you do not need to do anything other than select the box and insert the length of the ramp. The ramp is usually short; with ordinary bits, I set it to the bit diameter or a little less, so, in this project, I set it to 0.125" (3mm). (See Chapter 3 for an exception.)

Editing the Tools

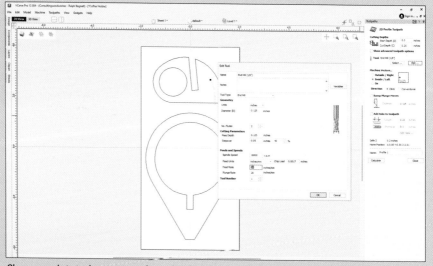

Changes made to tool parameters when using the Edit button are applied for this program only and revert back the next time you select the tool.

When you select a tool from the Tool Database, the CAD/CAM program will automatically use the settings already saved. Sometimes you may want to change the feed rate, pass depth, or another parameter, but only for that specific program. If you change the parameters in the Tool Database, they will be used on all future programs unless you change them again.

Instead of adjusting the settings in the Tool Database, click on the Edit button for temporary settings (pictured above). The Edit dialog box resembles the settings in the full database, but any changes you make will be applied only to the program you're currently working on. The next time you select the tool, it will default back to the Tool Database parameters.

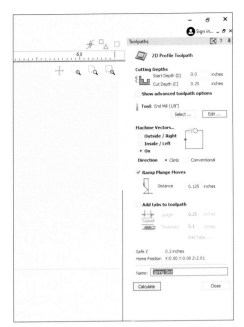

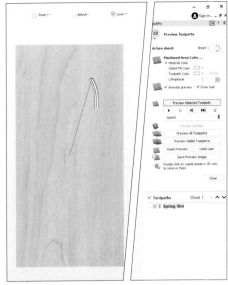

11 **Name your toolpaths.** This single line cut does not separate any parts from the stock, so no tabs are needed, and you can finish by naming the toolpath. The software will always provide a default name, but it would be "Profile 1," "Profile 2," and so on. Get into the habit now of naming your own toolpaths. Enter whatever name you want and finish by clicking on the Calculate button at the bottom.

12 **Review your CAD/CAM software for any errors.** Your program will show you the toolpath just created as a 3D model, as in Chapter 1. Click on Preview Selected Toolpath to see a representation of the actual cut. In this case, the cut is through the material, so the preview shows the background color through the new slot. If everything looks right on your screen, close the preview box and select the 2D tab at the top left corner of the workspace to start the next toolpath.

13 **Select the Inside/Left option within the profile toolpath to tell the program to cut inside the selected lines.** Select either of the inside circles on your drawing; they should both turn red because they are a group. Click on the Profile Toolpath icon again. Note that many inputs remain the same from the previous setup, so we only need to enter anything that will be different. Verify each choice as you work through the list; the cut depth and tool will remain the same as before. Under Machine Vectors, select the Inside/Left option. This tells the software that you want the bit to cut to the inside of these closed vectors. The program will automatically offset the bit by half its diameter so it will cut right up to the lines, but not over them. This keeps the opening in the part at the size drawn. You can see this in the small diagram on the right side of the dialog box. As before, leave the direction on Climb. The Ramp Plunge Moves check box defaults to deselected with the new toolpath, so be sure to select it now. The distance for the ramp remains the same because the bit is the same.

Setting Up Tabs

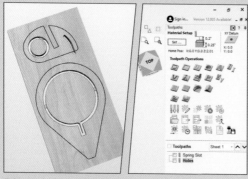

Tabs are the material left behind in the cut, so make sure they will be thick enough to hold.

Setting up tabs for your parts is pretty straightforward, but there are a few things to keep in mind as you choose the length and thickness of the tabs. The bit exerts side pressure on the stock as it is cutting. Bigger bits, deeper cuts, and faster feed speeds increase this side pressure, so you may need more tabs or stronger tabs to ensure they do not break. In this project, you are cutting thin stock with a narrow bit, so two small tabs are sufficient, but you need to be careful about the thickness. If your stock is thinner than set (0.23" instead of the 0.25" specified) then your tabs will also be thinner by the same amount. If your stock tends to run thin, increasing the thickness of the tabs will help keep everything in place.

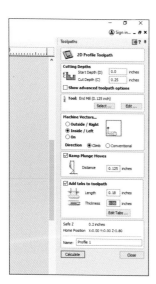

14 **Add tabs to the program to secure the parts that will be cut away.** This toolpath will separate the center cutouts out from the main stock. These are waste, but they need to be held in place so they are not thrown from the machine, injuring you or damaging the bit or the stock. One way to do this is with tabs. Tabs are "bridges" that remain uncut between the main stock and the tabbed item. The software will use your inputs to automatically leave these tabs behind when cutting the toolpath. You will need to cut them away and sand them smooth to separate the parts after the program is complete. Click on the Add Tabs to Toolpath box to select tabs, and two input boxes will be highlighted. The first is for the length of the tab side to side along the line. The second box is for how thick the left-behind tab should be. You want the tabs to be strong enough to hold the part but small enough to be easy to remove later. Here, I have selected a length of about ³⁄₁₆" (5mm) and a thickness of 0.06" (1.5mm) thick. Fill in these boxes, then click on the Edit Tabs button to see how they are placed.

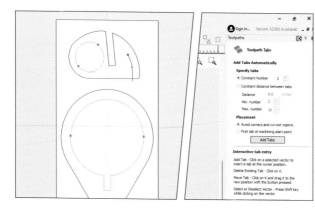

15 **Edit the tabs, if needed.** A new dialog box will open for you to edit the tabs. You can place tabs by number around the lines by spacing between tabs or even placing them manually. Click on Constant Number and input 2. Click on Add Tabs, and the program will place two tabs, evenly spaced, around both vectors. Click on Close at the bottom of the dialog box to finish the toolpath.

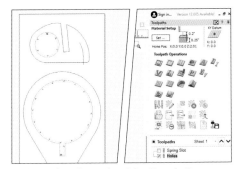

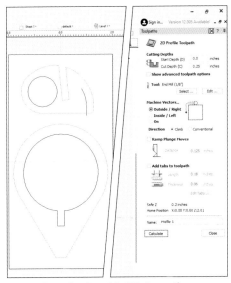

16 **Review the toolpath in 2D and 3D previews.** Type in a name for your toolpath and click on Calculate to finish it. Before clicking on Preview Selected Toolpath when the 3D preview opens, select 2D at the top left of the work area. With the small box checked next to the toolpath name on the right, you should see your selected closed vectors in red and the actual path of the center of the bit pictured as a gray line, with arrows showing the direction of the cut. You can clearly see that the gray line is offset from the line to be cut. This is because you selected the Inside/Left option under Machine Vectors earlier. Now click back on 3D and preview the toolpath. Note that in the 3D view, there is no visual difference between the cuts inside the line and the cuts on the line; you can only see it in the 2D preview with the toolpaths checked. Close the preview box, click on 2D again, and you can program the final cutting for your drink holder.

17 **Select the Outside/Right option within the profile toolpath to tell the program to cut the outside profile of the parts.** Click on the outside lines for either part, and both should change to red lines as a group. Select the Profile Toolpath icon again and work down through the choices. The cut depth and bit remain the same, but under Machine Vectors, click on the Outside/Right option. Like the Inside/Left option you just used, this also tells the program to offset the bit, but this time to the outside of the lines.

18 **Add tabs to the toolpath manually.** Click on the box for Ramp Plunge Moves and keep the same 0.125" (3mm) distance setting. Click on the Add Tabs to Toolpath box, keep the length and thickness numbers the same as before, and click on Edit Tabs. This time, you will add the tabs manually. Simply move your cursor over any part of the selected lines and click to add a tab. I prefer to place tabs on straight sections where possible, as they are the easiest to cut and sand. Outside curves are OK when there are limited straight areas to use, but avoid inside curves and slots because they are harder to clean up after milling. Note that I have used two tabs per part; one will simply not keep the part from moving. You can add another tab along the top arc of the lower part if you'd like. While you are learning your machine, having to clean up an extra tab or two is better than having a part that does not stay in place and gets ruined. As you gain experience, you will learn what works best for your setup. Close the Edit Tab dialog box, name the toolpath, and click on the Calculate button as before.

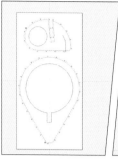 

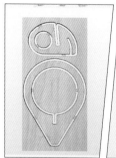 

19 **Review the outside of the part lines in the toolpath in 2D preview.** Before previewing the toolpath, click on 2D at the top left of the work area so you can again see the selected vectors and the actual toolpath. Note that this time the tool is offset outside the lines, so the overall size of the parts will be as drawn. Look closely, and you can even see markings where the tabs will be. All three of the toolpaths you created in this program are profile toolpaths, and by selecting On, Inside, or Outside, you choose how the bit will cut in reference to the selected lines.

20 **Click on 3D to return and preview the new toolpath.** If all three are not showing, click on Preview All Toolpaths, and you will see what your plywood blank should look like after milling.

Safety First

The two clamps that come with most machines are not sufficient to hold most projects, so consider buying or making more. I feel that four clamps are a minimum for safety.

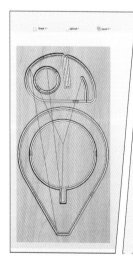 

21 **Save all three toolpaths.** All three of the toolpaths in this project use the same bit, so they are saved as a single G-code. Click on the small box next to Toolpaths at the bottom of the CAM sidebar to check the boxes for all three toolpaths you just created. Then click on Save Toolpath, which is the lower right icon in the stack. This opens a new dialog box. Working from the top down, choose Output All Visible Toolpaths to One File, then check to see that your three named toolpaths are listed below Toolpaths to Be Saved. If not, make sure they are checked; they are visible just below this dialog box. Your machine's post processor should be already entered because you set it up previously, so click on the Save Toolpath(s) button. Choose the folder where you want to save the G-code and give it a name that you will remember. Don't forget to save the CAD/CAM file as well before closing it and preparing to start your CNC machine.

X-Zero, Y-Zero

Because the program cuts the parts out from a larger piece of stock, the X-zero, Y-zero origin point set at the start does not need to be highly precise. The blank size allows for some tolerance, but the parts will still be the exact size specified.

Naming Programs

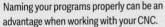

Naming your programs properly can be an advantage when working with your CNC.

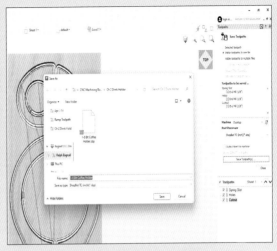

Pendants can simplify CNC operation, but they require special file names to work with their limited screen size.

Generally speaking, it is a good idea to name your programs so that you can readily find them again if needed, but some CNC machines require a bit more thought. CNCs are usually controlled by a separate computer, like the ShopBot I use in Chapter 1, or by a pendant, like the Axiom machine I use. The pendant has the advantage of allowing the machine to run independently of the computer, but the trade-off is a screen that only shows six characters of the program name. Modern computers allow for long file names, but you will need to think about how they appear on the pendant screen. Naming programs "KD Tray Cut" and "KD Tray Carve" will look fine on the computer, but when opened on the pendant, both show as "KD Tra-1." For pendant machines, I start file names with a number to show what order to run them in, followed by an abbreviation for the bit used, then any actual project names. So "KD Tray Carve" and "KD Tray Cut" become "1 V90 KD Tray Carve" and "2 116 KD Tray Cut," which appear on the screen as "1 V90-1" and "2 116-1," so I can tell the machine which order to run them in, and I know which bit to use for each one.

22 **Set up your CNC machine the same way you did in Chapter 1.** Mount the ⅛" (3mm) bit into the router collet and secure your stock onto the machine bed. This program will cut through the plywood stock, so you need to put a spoil board under it to protect the machine bed from damage. I used clamps to secure the stock to the machine bed. Mark the center point of your plywood, position the bit over the mark, and zero the X- and Y-axes. Set the Z-zero to the top of the stock manually as described in Chapter 1 or use a touch plate if your machine has one. With the three axes set, call up the G-code.

23 **Begin running your CNC program.** For safety, before you start the program, make sure you know where the bit will go first, so you are ready to stop the machine if it goes somewhere else. Start the run, and the first cut will be the spring slot toolpath you created, so the bit should move from the center of the part (X-zero and Y-zero) up and to the right as shown on the preview when programming. If the bit goes somewhere else, pause or stop the program and figure out the issue. The machine will move up to the end of the slot, and the bit will lower to the top of the stock, cut a short ramp into the stock, and then cut the curved line at ⅛" (3mm) deep. It will then make a second pass at ¼" (6mm) deep, cutting through the stock and slightly into the spoil board below. Listen to the sound of the cutting. If the bit seems to be struggling, you may need to pause the program and reduce the feed rate. If it sounds like it is cutting easily, you may be able to raise the feed rate for this bit in your Tool Database for future programs.

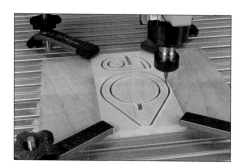

24 **Continue running your CNC program to cut your parts.** After finishing the slot, the bit will rise above the stock and move to begin the second toolpath, cutting out the center holes. These also begin with a ramp and a ⅛" (3mm) deep first cut. Watch closely, and, as the second cut is made, you will see the bit rise slightly at the points along the path where the tabs are left behind. When both holes are cut out, the bit rises again and moves to cut the outside profiles. Watch as the two parts are cut from the plywood blank, and you will again see the tabs being left behind.

25 **Cut the tabs to separate the drink holder sections.** Unclamp the plywood stock from the machine bed. If the tabs worked, your two parts are still connected to the rest of the blank. Separate the drink holder sections by cutting the tabs close to the edges of the part, being careful not to cut into the parts themselves. Your tabs should be thin enough to cut with a utility knife.

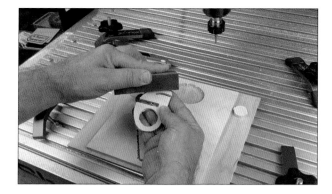

26 **Sand and add finish to the parts.** Using the right bit with good-quality materials should create cleanly cut parts, but finish sanding is always needed. Sand off the rest of the tabs first, then ease all the edges with a fine grit sanding. Finish the parts with a simple coat of wax or a clear coat of polyurethane or shellac.

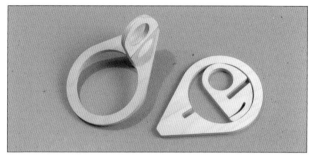

27 **Slide the slots on each part over one another.** Your drink holder was designed to come apart and store flat, making it ideal for holding hot drinks when traveling. The handle fits into the hole in the body, and the spring tab is compressed slightly to help hold it in place—all made using just the Profile Toolpath commands!

Stock Options for Projects

Craft stores, hobby shops, and discount stores, as well as specialty woodworking stores, will have parts you can use.

Not every CNC owner is a woodworker or has a full workshop where they can prepare whatever stock they need for their projects. So, the projects in this book have been designed to use readily available materials that can be bought online or at a local shop and need little to no preparation before cutting.

Your local craft store will have unfinished wood plaques that can be carved. Hobby shops that sell radio-control models will have the sort of high-quality thin plywood used for the drink holder in Chapter 2. Woodworking stores sell all sorts of wood species in many sizes and thicknesses, both in store and online, so you can easily get the material needed for the tic-tac-toe board in Chapter 3. Amazon and other online sources offer a huge selection of small wood blanks in many sizes and shapes. I would be surprised if you couldn't find the stock you needed in the sizes you want.

CHAPTER 3

TIC-TAC-TOE BOARD

This project introduces drawing simple shapes within the CAD/CAM program that you will combine for milling using the Pocket Toolpath to create holes and pockets. This project also uses more than one bit to introduce you to working with tool changes and multiple G-codes.

Supplies

- 5" (125mm) x 9" (225mm) x ¾" (19mm) cherry, beech, or other tight-grain wood stock
- ¼" (6mm) straight bit (Freud 74-206 or similar)
- ½" (12mm) diameter dish carving bit (Freud #19-104 or similar)

Skill Building

In this project, you will:

- Use the drawing features of the CAD/CAM software.
- Move and manipulate drawn features.
- Use an array to create multiple items.
- Add a form tool in the Tool Database.
- Create holes without drilling.
- Hold parts by programming an onion skin cutout.
- Cut the project using multiple router bits.

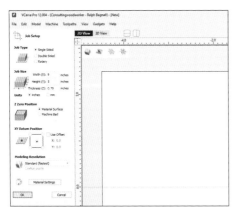

1 Set up the size of the job. You will draw this project in the CAD/CAM software, so there is no file to open. Select New Project on the main screen of your software and enter the parameters in the Job Setup dialog box. Enter the stock size as 9" (230mm) x 5" (130mm) by ¾" (19mm) thick. Set the Z-zero to Material Surface and select the center of the stock as the XY datum position. Click on OK at the bottom of the window to begin drawing the game board.

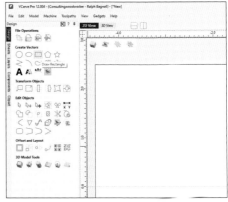

2 Select the Draw Rectangle icon. Drawing is done by first using the various commands under the Create Vectors category. This group of icons allows you to draw circles, rectangles, other shapes, lines, and other objects you will need. For this project, start by selecting the Draw Rectangle icon and filling in the information required in the dialog box.

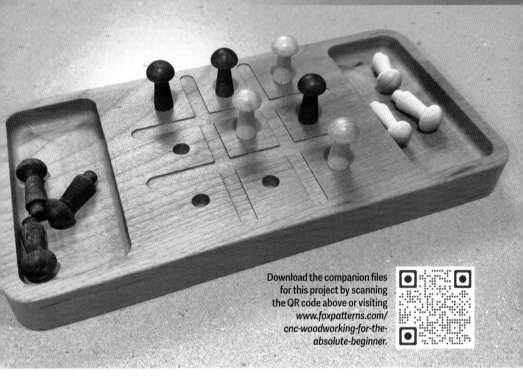

Drawing and Layout Options

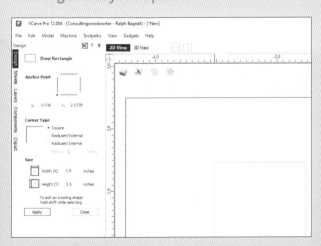

Positioning your drawn elements in the workspace depends on the Anchor Point you choose in the Drawing dialog box. You can draw elements exactly where you want them if you already know all the measurements. In many cases, though, the software makes it easier to create objects anywhere and then position them where you want them based on their relationship to the workspace or to other objects in the drawing. You will do this using the Transform Objects commands throughout Chapter 3.

It is sometimes more efficient to place drawn objects by their relationships to other items rather than by using exact X, Y coordinates.

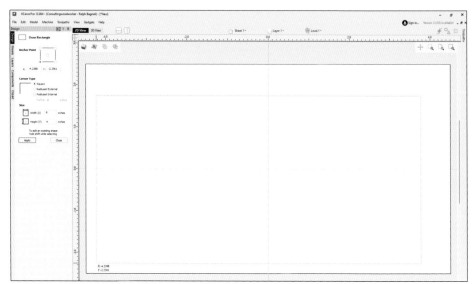

3 **Create the rectangle for the game board cutout path.** Start creating the game board by selecting the Anchor Point icon at the lower left in the dialog box. Then enter the size you want for your rectangle in the boxes at the bottom of the dialog box: 8" (200mm) for the width (X-axis) and 4" (100mm) for the height (Y-axis). Clicking anywhere in the lower left area of the workspace creates the rectangle in the size you chose. Close the dialog box, then click on the Align Selected Objects icon. In the box that opens, click the top center icon to place the rectangle in the exact center of the workspace. This will be the game board cutout path.

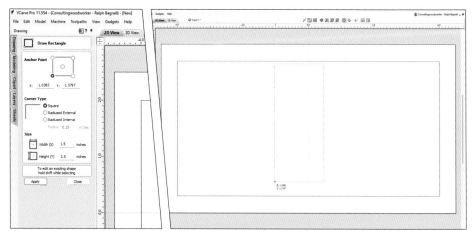

4 **Draw and center a second rectangle inside the first one.** Open the Draw Rectangle box again and enter 1.5" (40mm) for the width (X-axis) and 3.5" (90mm) for height (Y-axis). Click anywhere within the workspace to create the rectangle. Center this rectangle in the workspace using the Align Selected Objects command as you did with the larger rectangle.

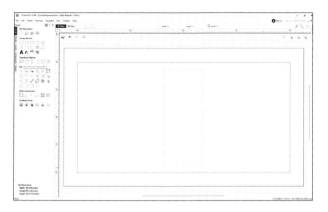

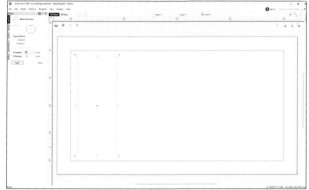

5 **Move the smaller rectangle to the left of the game board.** Click on the Move Selected Objects icon within the Transform Objects category. This will open up a new dialog box for repositioning the selected item(s). In this dialog box, you can move the selected object(s) to an Absolute position, meaning to exact X and Y coordinates, or to a Relative position, which means moving it in X and/or Y by a distance you choose. Click on the circle marked Relative to move the rectangle by a chosen distance and in a chosen direction. The smaller rectangle is 1.5" (40mm) wide and is centered on the 8" (200mm) game board. To position it so it is ¼" (6mm) from the edge, you need to move it -3" (-75mm) to the left, which is in the X-axis. In the Cartesian coordinate system the CNC uses, moving from right to left is a negative move.

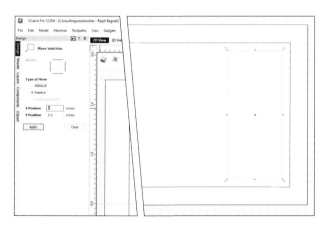

6 **Create a second smaller rectangle and move to the right of the game board.** The second rectangle should also be 1.5" (40mm) by 3.5" (90mm). Then center the rectangle on the workspace, and move it 3" (75mm) to the right side of the game board. Moving it from left to right in the X axis is a positive move, so enter 3" (75mm) dimension in the positive.

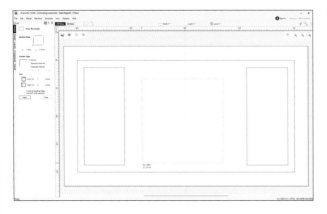

7 **Create and center the playing field boundaries on the game board.** The lines dividing the playing field will be 3.5" (90mm) long, but they will be cut on the lines with a ¼" (6mm) bit, so the lines need to be shorter by the bit diameter. Create a 3.25" (82mm) square and center it on the game board to create the boundaries of the playing field.

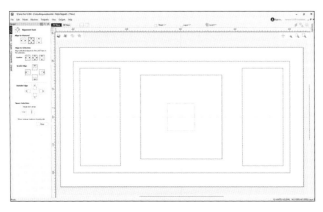

8 **Create the tic-tac-toe grid.** Create a 1.125" (28mm) square and center it on the project in the same way as with the rectangles. This is the center box within the four lines that make the tic-tac-toe grid. This box within the larger game box makes it easy to create the lines needed for routing the grid.

Drawing in a Snap

You can start any line or object by entering the X, Y positions you want in the dialog box for the object, but you may not know the exact point. All CAD/CAM programs allow for **snapping** to a nearby known point. You may have noticed the cursor changing appearance or even moving on its own when you move it near an existing object or origin point—this is snapping. The software recognizes that most new elements will be drawn from origin points, corners, or centers of existing objects. When you move the cursor close to any of these points, it will position itself exactly on the point to ensure it is aligned and show the exact X, Y coordinates. The **snap** settings are usually turned on by default, and you can turn them on or off as needed. Using the snap features can save time by allowing you to skip a lot of math and just work from existing points.

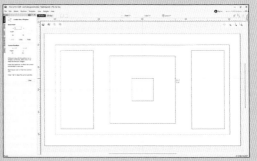

Snapping is a feature in all CAD programs that can automatically help your cursor locate important points in the drawing.

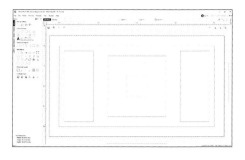

9 Open the dialog box to draw the lines for the game board. Click on the Draw Line/Polyline icon within the Create Vectors icons. This will open a new dialog box where you will enter the information needed to draw lines. It is easier to create the lines for the game board by working from the last two rectangles you created. You know that all four lines extend from the small square to the larger outer square drawn in the center of the game board, and you can use this to quickly and accurately create the lines needed.

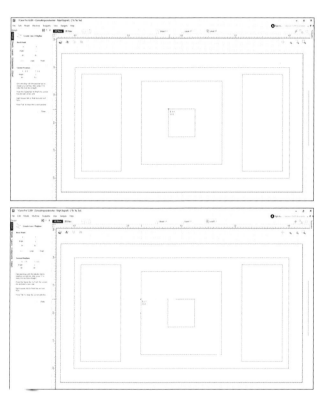

10 Draw the first line. Enter the start point of the first horizontal line of the tic-tac-toe board in Next Point at the top of the Create Line/Polyline dialog box. This line should start at X -1.625" (-41mm), Y 0.562" (14mm), but you do not need to figure this out on your own; the software can help. This first horizontal line will extend across the top of the small box. Move your cursor close to the top left of the box, and it will snap to the corner and display the coordinates. This is the snap feature, and it can do more. Move your cursor straight out to the left from the corner, and you should see a dotted line following it, telling you that the cursor is aligned along the X-axis. When your cursor reaches the outer box, it should snap onto the side; if the dotted line is still following the cursor, this is the point where you want the new line to start. Note that it shows X -1.625" (-41mm), Y 0.562" (14mm) which is where you wanted your line to start. Click to anchor the start point of your line at this location.

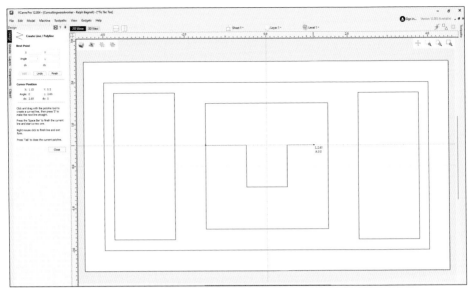

11 **Draw the second line.** Move your cursor to the right, and a dotted line will extend from the start point, again following the cursor as it travels. As you move the mouse, you may see other lines forming from other points on the drawing, trying to connect with the cursor. The software is suggesting different relationships from which you can choose to create items. Move the cursor straight across the top of the small box until it snaps to the right side of the larger box. Click here to end the line. Because this is a polyline creation tool, the end point of the first line becomes the start point of the next. You may want to use this feature at some point, but these lines need to be independent. End the line by right-clicking the mouse or hitting the escape key.

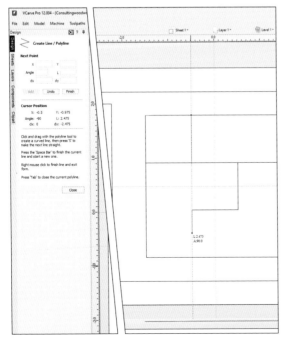

12 **Draw the remaining lines.** Create the other horizontal line in the same way, aligned with the bottom of the small square. Then create the vertical lines: hover over the small square's corner, move the cursor until it snaps to the top of the larger square, draw it downward to the bottom, and repeat for the second vertical line. Note that each time you end a line, the dialog box disappears, and you will need to reopen it. You can do this by clicking on the icon again. In many programs, clicking the spacebar is a shortcut that will reopen that last command used.

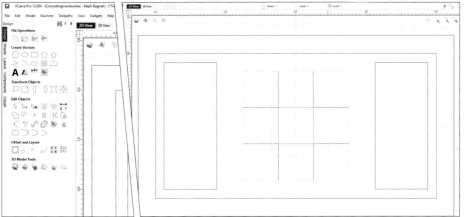

13 **Delete the two square boxes in the lines of the tic-tac-toe board.** The outer one is easy: just click anywhere on it to highlight it. The inner box is hidden under the lines you just drew, so click and hold your mouse above and to the left of the box, then drag it below and to the right. If you include all of the small box, but not all of the lines, only the box will be selected, you should see the dotted red lines of the box. Delete both in preparation for drawing the circles.

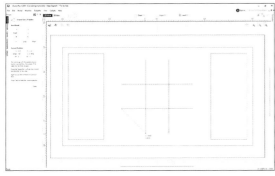

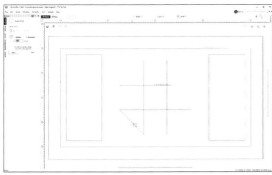

14 **Draw a small circle in the center of each game piece.** These circles are drawn because the tic-tac-toe board uses pegs to mark the game play. These circles will be cut as pockets to hold the pegs. Open the Create Line/Polyline command again and draw a line diagonally across the lower left corner square. The center point of this line is where you want the center of the circle to be. Click on the Draw Circle icon, and a new dialog box will open. You can specify the location of the circle using dimensions, but the snap feature again comes in handy here. Leave the Center Point boxes blank and enter the diameter of the circle. The pegs used are ¼" in diameter (6.4mm), so make the circles 0.26" (6.5mm) so the pegs will fit, even if they are a bit oversized. Hover the mouse near the center of the new diagonal line, and the cursor should snap to the right spot: the center point of the line. Click the mouse and create the new circle. Then click on the diagonal line and delete it.

Arrays

You could draw the other eight circles, but using the Array Copy commands found under Offset and Layout on the left-hand menu box is easier. An array is a command that can make multiple copies of an object in a pattern you define. It can be a row (a line of objects in Y), a column (a line of objects in X), or a grid of objects in both X and Y. There are other icons for making copies around a circle, like bolt holes, and even along a path that you draw, but in this case, you will create a grid of circles.

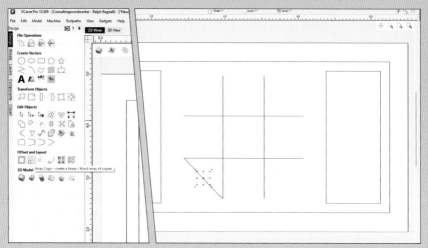

Arrays are a shortcut for laying out multiple items in a regular pattern, like the tic-tac-toe holes.

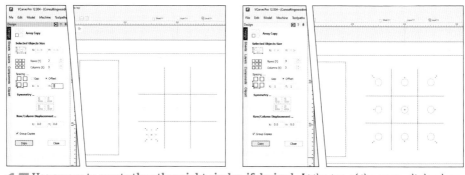

15 **Use arrays to create the other eight circles, if desired.** At the top of the array dialog box is the size of the selected object. You won't add to or change this data, but it is helpful for figuring out the spacing to array the objects correctly. Enter the number of rows (Y) and/or columns (X) you want to lay out. You need nine holes, so type in 3 rows and 3 columns. Next, choose how the spacing is determined by clicking on Gap or Offset. Gap is the spacing between objects, and each object's size needs to be figured into the array's final size. Offset is the spacing between points within the objects and ignores the objects' size. Selecting either shows a small graphic illustrating the difference. Your circles need to be spaced according to their centers, so click on Offset. The spacing does not always need to be the same in X and Y, but in this case, it is. Remember that the game play lines are 1.125" (28mm) apart in both X and Y, so enter that number in the boxes provided. Symmetry and Displacement are not needed for this project, so leave them alone. Click on Copy at the bottom of the dialog box, which should give you a grid of nine holes, one in the center of each space on the board.

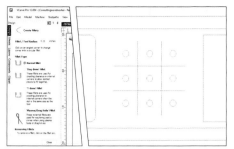
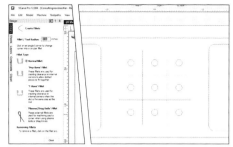

16 **Round the pockets and corners of the game board with fillets.** The pockets on either side of the game board will be cut out using a ½" (12mm) router bit. Router bits cannot create square inside corners because they will always be rounded by the radius of the bit, so these will be ¼" (6mm). If you leave the vectors square, they will still have a ¼" (6.4mm) radius in each corner, which you will see when you preview the toolpath. Adding the radius to the drawing makes it easier to set the outside corner radius next. Type 0.25" (6mm) into the Fillet/Tool Radius box and select the Normal Fillet circle. Move the cursor to each corner of the pocket, and when the cursor image shows a check mark or otherwise changes, click. This will redraw the square corner with the proper curve. Radius the corners of both pockets to the 0.25" (6mm) dimension. Round the corners of the game board itself using the same technique. In most cases, it looks better if adjacent corners are rounded to be evenly spaced around the curve. The corner inside the pocket is 0.25" (6mm), and it is ¼" (6mm) from the edge. Setting the outer radius to be 0.50" (12mm) will make the two concentric, which is usually what we expect to see. With the fillets completed, group the objects before beginning the toolpath work.

Fillets

At this point, you've drawn all the needed objects, but the boxes all have square corners, and the game board should have smooth corners for comfort. The Fillet icon is a quick and easy way to round off sharp corners to whatever radius you need.

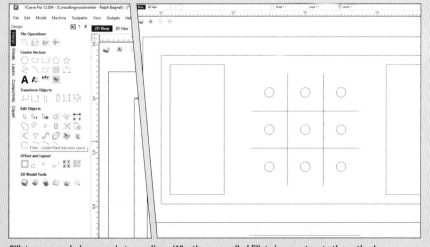

Fillets are rounded corners between lines. Why they are called fillets is a mystery to the author!

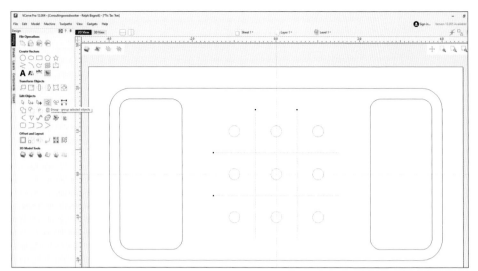

17 **Group items for similar cut profiles.** Group similar objects by selecting them and then clicking on the Group Selected Objects icon. Remember that selected objects show as red dashed lines until they are grouped, and grouped objects show as solid red lines. Clicking on any one of the grouped objects will select or deselect them all at once. Group the objects as you will toolpath them. Group all the circles because they will use the Pocket Toolpath and be cut to the same depth. Group the lines and group the two pockets because the objects in each group will be cut the same way. Grouping saves time over selecting everything individually, and grouping also ensures that no items are missed. Your completed drawing is ready to be toolpathed, so click on Toolpaths at the top of the page to switch to the Toolpath commands.

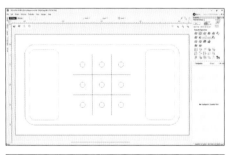

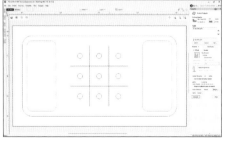

18 **Create a pocket toolpath to remove material within the closed vectors.** Pocket toolpaths are different from the profile toolpaths you used to cut to the inside of the drink holder in Chapter 2. The profile toolpath cuts only along the border, leaving any excess material within the vector uncut. The pocket toolpath starts in the center of the closed vector and automatically plans a path for the tool to cut everything it can reach inside the borders. This is the best choice for creating pockets like those on your tic-tac-toe board. Select the pockets on your drawing and click on the Pocket Toolpath icon. Work your way through the Pocket Toolpath dialog box, entering the required information as you did with the Profile Toolpath dialog box. The pockets will start at the top of the stock and be cut 0.375" (9.5mm) deep, so set Start Depth to 0 and Cut Depth to 0.375" (9.5mm).

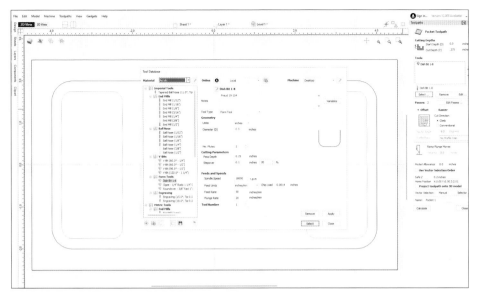

19 **Apply the dish carving bit from your Tool Database.** You can cut these pockets with a straight bit, but a dish carving bit has round, instead of square, corners. It will create a flat-bottomed pocket with a radius along the lower edges, making them easier to clean. (These types of pockets are very useful on toys and serving dishes.) You will need to create the dish carving bit in your Tool Database if you have not already; see the sidebar on page 55. Select the ⅛" (3mm) dish carving bit and click Apply.

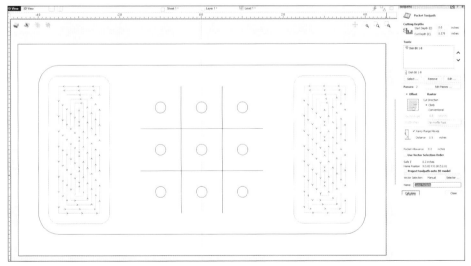

20 **Calculate the pocket toolpath.** Working down the Pocket Toolpath dialog box, choose Offset for the path, which will start in the center and cut to the pocket edges. As always, click on the Ramp Toolpath box. This bit is not really designed to plunge, so instead of the usual half of the bit diameter, make the ramp length the full diameter or even a bit more. The longer ramp length will ease the bit into the material with less stress. Name the toolpath and click on Calculate.

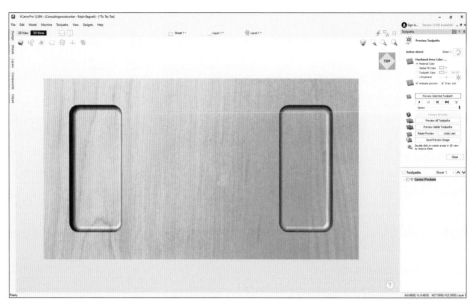

21 **Preview the pockets.** Using the Preview Toolpaths function, the pockets show up on the board. The radius is easily seen where the bottom meets the sides. This appears in the preview because you set up the bit that way. It takes more time to set up these specialized form tools, but they are a great help in designing and programming your projects.

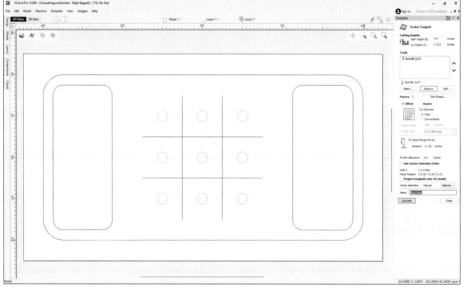

22 **Program the holes for the pegs.** Select them and click on the Pocket Toolpath icon again. Set Cut Depth to 0.312" (8mm), just a little deeper than the pins on the game pegs. Select a ¼" (6mm) end mill to cut the holes. You drew the holes at 0.26" (6.5mm), so they can be cut using a ¼" (6mm) straight bit without burning.

Creating Form Tools

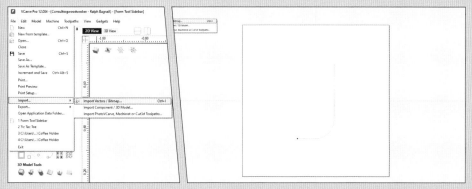

Add your bits to the Tool Database to see them properly in the preview function.

Finish creating your custom tool by adding the cutting parameters like you would with any bit.

VCarve and other CAD/CAM software often come with a basic set of tools (router bits) preloaded in the Tool Database, and these will be enough to get you started on most projects. This tic-tac-toe board requires a slightly unusual bit that is not part of the typical database, so let's look at how you can add specialty bits to your database.

Tools like straight, V, and ball nose bits are usually included in the database and can be adapted for your bits and machine. This tic-tac-toe project uses a dish carving bit that is not included, so you will enter it as a **form tool**. The Form Tool category of bits allows you to use profile router bits like this dish carving bit and show the bit profile on your parts in the 3D preview so you can see how they will come out before cutting any wood.

Adding a form tool to your database requires a drawing of the bit's shape; in this case, a drawing of the right half of the bit from the center line to the top of the cutter. With this dish carving bit, this is a horizontal line ⅛" (3.2mm) long, with a ⅛" (3.2mm) radius corner, leading to a horizontal line ⅜" (9.5mm) tall. The drawing for this tool is labeled "Dish Bit.dxf" in the download package for this book.

Open a new CAD/CAM project and set Job Size to 1" (25mm) by 1" (25mm). Import Dish Bit.dxf from the download files (or draw it yourself as you would any job). Select the vectors and combine them as you usually do with imports. Then switch to the CAM side of the software, make sure the profile in the work area is selected, and then open the Tool Database dialog box. Click on Add Tool at the bottom left of the window.

VCarve will default to one of the preloaded bits as you start. Select the Form Tool option from the Tool Type drop-down menu below the Notes section. The computer will automatically create the tool shape if it is selected and drawn correctly and will display it to the right of the database window. It will also fill in a name for the bit as well as its diameter. You can rename the bit now if you want. Next, fill in the number of flutes (typically 2) and click Create Settings. The software will fill out the rest of the form.

It is a good idea to always review these settings because you want them to conform to your machine, especially the pass depth and feed rate. Add the manufacturer and model number of your specialty bit to the Notes section so you can always find the right replacement. Click on Apply to save the new tool in your Tool Database.

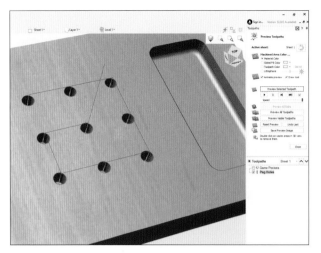

23 **Preview the peg holes.** The holes must be bigger than the bit so the software can interpolate the hole, spiraling the bit downward rather than drilling straight in. A bit spinning at 14,000 RPM cannot just plunge straight in like a drill bit at 600 RPM because it will burn the wood and ruin the bit. Set the ramp distance to 0.125" (3mm), rename the toolpath so you will remember it, and click Calculate to create the toolpath.

Pocket Toolpath Uses

There are other uses for pocket toolpaths; for example, you can fully cut small circles or openings, so the chips are removed by the dust collector rather than having tabs that need to be cut and sanded smooth. It may take a little longer on the machine, but it saves you a lot of work after milling.

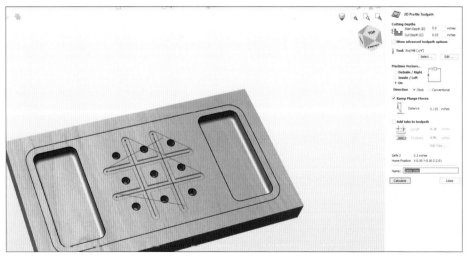

24 **Program the tic-tac-toe lines.** The rest of the program is done with profile toolpaths. The tic-tac-toe lines are next, and they are simple to set up by working down the toolpath list. These are shallow lines, so set the depth to 0.03" (1mm), and they will be cut with the same ¼" (6mm) end mill as the holes. Set the Machine Vectors to On so the cuts will be centered along the lines. While this cut is shallow enough that it probably does not need to be ramped, ramping all cuts is still a good habit. Type in 0.06" (1.5mm) to save a bit of time. Name the toolpath and click on Calculate.

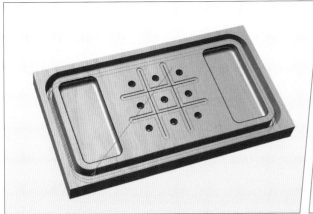

25 **Finish programming the game board.** It only remains to cut the game board out, again using the ¼" (6mm) bit. Set Cut Depth to 0.72" (18mm) deep. This will cut most of the way through the stock, leaving a thin layer at the bottom to hold the game in place. This is called an onion skin, and it is an alternative to the tabs used to hold the parts in Chapter 2. Choose Outside for the Machine Vectors here and set the ramp to the typical half of the tool diameter, 0.125" (3mm). Name the toolpath and click Calculate. The preview should now show the entire game board. Note that the bottom of the cutout shows the onion skin left behind.

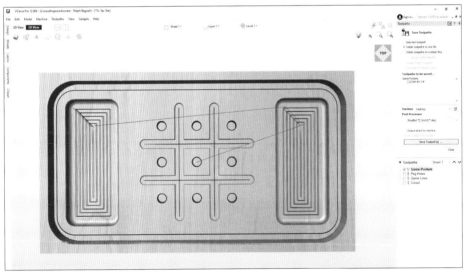

26 **Save the toolpaths using the dish carving bit.** This program uses two different router bits, so you will need to save it as two different G-code files. Close out of preview mode and click on the Save Toolpath icon at the bottom right of the workspace. Under Toolpaths, click on the box next to Game Pockets. This is the only one using the dish carving bit, so you need to save it as a G-code by itself. As before, the file name defaults to the toolpath name, but get into the habit of naming it so you will know what it does and what bit to use. For a pendant machine, call this "1-8 Dish Pocket" to indicate the bit and purpose in the first few characters. For PC machines, you will see the whole file name, so call the G-code anything you will remember.

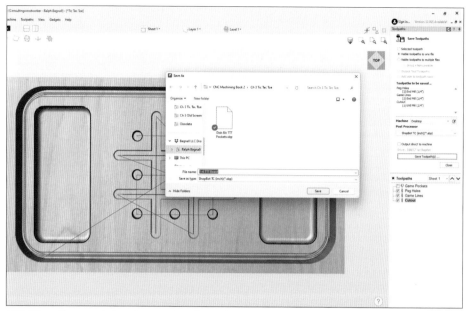

27 **Save the remaining three toolpaths and secure workpiece to CNC machine.** The remaining three toolpaths all use the same bit, so even though they do very different tasks and use different toolpath types, they can all be saved as a single G-code. Check the boxes to select these three toolpath names and make sure that Pocket Toolpath is not selected. The software will not allow you to save a G-code that includes more than one bit. Save this G-code under a name that you choose. You are now ready to fire up the CNC and make your tic-tac-toe board. Turn on your CNC machine and get it ready to run according to the manual, as you've done previously. Secure the 9" (230mm) by 5" (130mm) stock onto the machine bed. Even though there will be no through cuts with the onion skin, it is safer to use a waste piece underneath.

Securing the Bit

Clamping your router bits securely into the collet is important not only to prevent the bit from slipping out of position and ruining your project but also because slipping will damage the collet and the shank of the bit. Tightening the collet properly starts with keeping it clean and removing debris so that nothing interferes with the hold on the bit. The shank of the bit must fill at least ¾ of the collet, and the nut should be secured without overtightening. If your router uses two wrenches, tighten them using one hand to secure the bit properly while allowing for removal without undue stress.

Tools must be firmly clamped in the spindle, but be careful not to overtighten them.

28 **Begin setting up the CNC machine.** Manually jog the head of the CNC until it is positioned over the center of the stock. A V bit is excellent for precisely setting the head location, but with this program it needs only to be close, not exact. Reset the X- and Y-axes to zero to start the program in the middle because that is where you set the start point in the software.

29 **Install the dish carving bit in the router and set the Z-axis height to the top of your stock.** As in Chapters 1 and 2, you can do this either manually with a piece of paper or using a touch plate if your machine has one. With all three axes zeroed, call up the dish carving bit G-code program and begin cutting.

30 **Cut the pockets.** Pay attention to the chips as the dish carving bit is cutting. If the speed and feed are set correctly, you should see big flakes of wood flying from the bit. If the cut is making mostly powder rather than flakes, then either the feed is too low, the RPM too fast, or both. Take note and change the bit settings for future use. Watching the results of your programs will help you get a feel for the best settings for your bits on your machine.

31 **Switch to the ¼" (6mm) straight bit for the second G-code program.** Inspect the bit and collet as you swap the cutters. Remove any debris or dust from the collet and nut to ensure a secure hold on the bit. The X-zero and Y-zero point must stay the same between bit changes, but the Z-axis height must be set for each tool used in the program. Forgetting this step is one of the most common mistakes, and it can easily ruin your project.

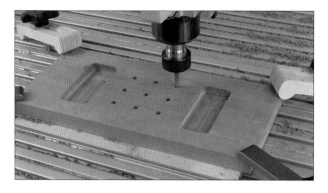

32 **Cut the peg holes.** Start the G-code you created for the ¼" (6mm) bit. This G-code includes three toolpaths, starting with the peg holes. As the bit cuts the holes, note how the bit is cutting downward in a tight spiral instead of just drilling straight in. This is the interpolation movement you programmed earlier to keep the bit cool and the stock from burning.

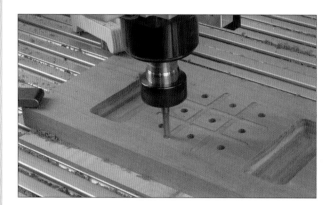

33 **Cut the lines of the game board.** These should be about ¹⁄₃₂" (1mm) deep and rounded at the ends, just like the bit. Nothing at this point should be much of a surprise because you verified everything in the preview function of your CAD/CAM software.

Smaller Can Be Better

CNC routers should not be used to drill holes like a drill press because the bits turn too fast and will cause burning. You are also limited in the diameters available. It is always better to use a smaller bit and let it cut the needed hole size. This means unlimited choices for hole diameter, so if you want to use different pegs for this game, you can just resize the holes and recalculate instead of reworking the entire toolpath.

The pegs used here have a nominal ¼" (6mm) stem, so the holes were created to be 0.26" (6.5mm) to allow a ¼" (6mm) bit to make the holes. If your pegs need smaller holes, you can switch to a ³⁄₁₆" (5mm) or even ⅛" (3mm) bit. This may require adapting some of the other tasks that the ¼" (6mm) was used for or even adding a tool change, but you'll get better results and extend your bit life.

Create cleaner holes and extend your bit life by using a bit that is smaller than the hole needed.

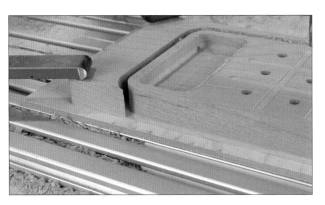

34 Cut the outside of the game board.

The program finishes by cutting the outside profile of your game board with the same ¼" (6mm) bit. Remember that you intentionally set the cut depth to leave a thin layer of material—the onion skin—behind. This is a very reliable method of keeping your part in place as the program finishes. It has the advantage over tabs in that the bit does not cut into your spoil board, and you won't need to cut away and sand the tabs.

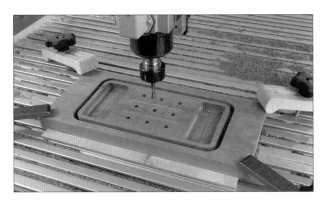

35 Remove the finished game board from the waste by cutting the onion skin with a hand router.

Your tic-tac-toe game is completed. Remove the part from the CNC bed, drill a ¼" (6mm) hole through the onion skin, then trim the skin away following the body of the game board with a flush trim bit. Lightly sand the entire game board and apply your favorite finish.

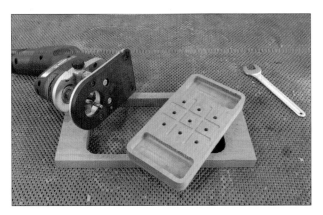

36 Personalize your game board and pieces, if desired.

These game boards can be personalized with a little carving in the bottom of the pockets. A set of inexpensive pegs become the game pieces. Stain or paint half of them to differentiate the two players.

CHAPTER 4

Garden Marker

Being able to carve text and engrave images is the main reason many people buy a CNC, so this project is designed to get you started programming V-carving/engraving toolpaths. You can use the garden marker for plants indoors or out, and you can use the same techniques to make all sorts of useful items from luggage tags to wall plaques.

Supplies

- 4" (100mm) x 7" (180mm) x ¼" (6mm) good-quality plywood
- 60-degree V bit (Whiteside 1540 or similar)
- ¼" (6mm) straight bit (Onsrud 57-910 or similar)

Skill Building

In this project, you will:
- Use the CAD/CAM software to create text for carving.
- Import and join vectors for toolpathing.
- Import drawings and use the Trace command to create usable vectors.
- Program text, drawing, and engraving using the V-carving toolpath.
- Use multiple router bits to complete the project.

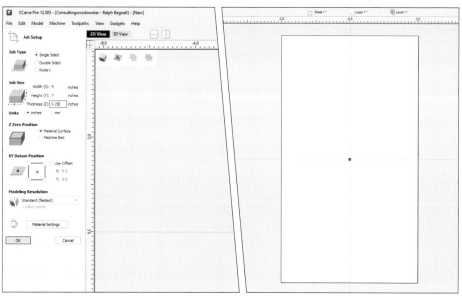

1 Set up the job. Begin by creating a new file and setting up the job at 4" (100mm) wide x 7" (180mm) tall. Set the thickness to ¼" (6mm), set the XY datum position (origin point) to the center of the panel, and deselect Use Offset. Click OK to close the dialog box and return to the work screen.

Download the companion files for this project by scanning the QR code above or visiting *www.foxpatterns. com/cnc- woodworking- for-the- absolute- beginner.*

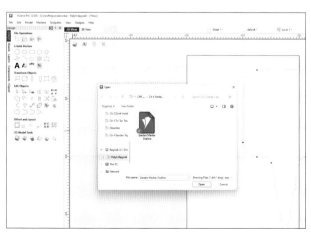

2 Import the vectors.
Click on Import Vectors and select the Garden Marker.dxf file in the file download for this book (available via the QR code above). Click Open to import the shape, select the entire outline, and center it on the workspace using the Center Objects command as you did in Chapter 3. If you want the practice, you can draw your own outline using the various Create Objects icons.

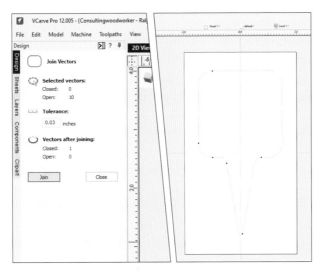

3 **Join the vectors.** Make sure that you've selected the entire outline, then click the Join Vectors icon to open the dialog box. You should see 0 Closed and 10 Open at the top under Selected Vectors. At the bottom of the dialog box, you should see 1 Closed and 0 Open where it says Vectors after Joining. If not, then increase the tolerance to 0.03" (0.7mm) or 0.04" (1mm). With only one vector showing, click on the Join button to connect the vectors, then close the dialog box.

True Type or Single Line Fonts?

Spinning router bits are not very well suited for making letters. No matter the profile, the end of each cut will be round, which is not ideal for most text. The V-carving/engraving subroutines that your CAD/CAM system uses for carving are designed to work within the outlines of letters, not following individual lines.

The font at the top of the image to the right is Times New Roman in True Type, and below is Times New Roman Single Line. With True Type, all characters, block or script, are made up of outlines that can be engraved into. Single Line fonts are just that: made up of single lines. Much of the script is made up of open vectors, which are rejected by the V-carving/engraving subroutine.

Single Line fonts are suitable for use with profile toolpaths and will not work with the V-Carving/Engraving Toolpath commands. Note how all the Single Line font letters end in rounded corners because the bit cuts in a circle. You should experiment with using Single Line fonts at some point, because they are certainly faster and very useful for marking and labeling, but you'll want True Type fonts for most projects.

True Type fonts are usually more suitable for carving and engraving text.

Single Line fonts will never have the sharp corners that mimic hand carving, but they still can be useful.

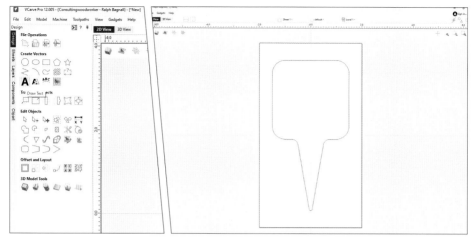

4 Draw the text dialog box. The next step is to create the text to be carved. Under the Create Vectors section of the menu on the left side, find the Draw Text icon and select it to open the text dialog box.

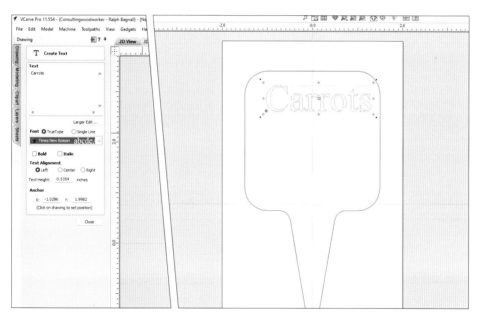

5 Add in the text for the markers. The text dialog box is used like most of the other dialog boxes, work from top to bottom, filling in the needed data or variables. At the top is a space to type your text. Type "Carrots" here (or whatever you want to plant) for this project. Use the Larger Text button if you are adding a lot of text, but remember that all text in the box will be treated the same. Select True Type font and use the drop-down menu to choose the font style to carve. The dropdown menu should show you the True Type fonts loaded on your computer from any source. Select Times New Roman. You have options to make your text bold or italic and to justify it left, center, or right, just like in a word processor. You can manually resize the text using the mouse, and you often can set up a bounding box to contain the text. Just like when drawing objects in Chapter 3, it is easiest to simply click on the workspace near where you want the text. The text (i.e., Carrots) will appear, and you can use the Transform Objects commands to place the text where you want.

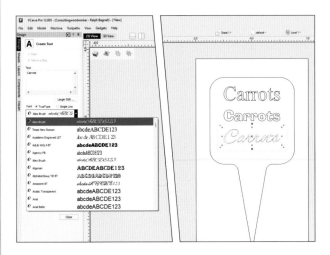

6 **Choose the font style for your markers.** After placing your text, you can experiment with different font styles and sizes to get the look you want. Just be careful to avoid fine or elaborate fonts, as fine lines make shallow cuts and can be hard to see. Experiment with using the bold and italic options as well, as they can provide more options for your project.

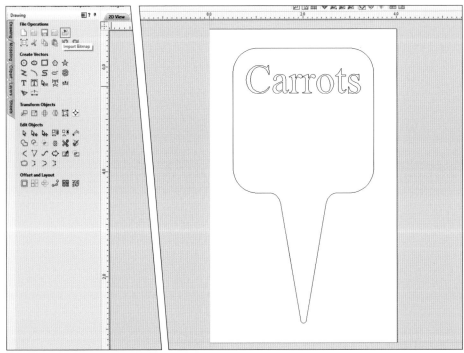

7 **Import images, if desired.** You can import clip art and other images just like DXF files into your software. You can import anything from line art to photos. The Import icon may not be the same in all software, but most CAD/CAM programs can import the same types of file formats. To use image files in your project, you must first convert them into vectors. All importable image files are referred to as bitmaps, or rasters in VCarve, no matter their actual file type. In this project, you will be working with a basic clip art image. Select the Carrot Clip Art file from the download files for this book (available via the QR code at the start of this chapter) and click Open to import it. Images will automatically be centered and resized to fit the workspace. In this case, the carrot image fills the workspace side to side, making it somewhat larger than needed. You can resize it using the Transform Objects commands or by manipulating it manually.

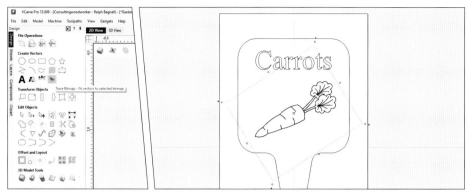

8 **Move and scale the images as desired.** The image is selected when it imports. Click on it when highlighted to activate the handles that allow you to manually work with the image. The small diamond outlines at each corner can be used to scale the image. Click on one and hold the mouse button down, then move the cursor in or out to make the image smaller or larger. Clicking and holding the diamond in the center of the image allows you to pan the image as a whole, moving it anywhere within the workspace. Clicking and holding the blue squares just outside the diamonds let you rotate the image. Use the mouse with these handles to fit the carrot image within the square below the text as shown in the image above.

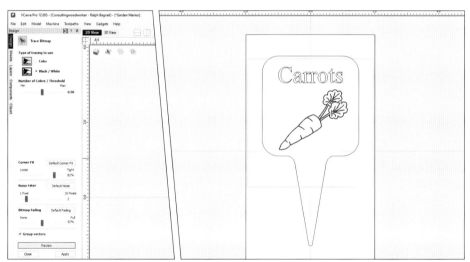

9 **Convert the imported images into vectors for use within toolpaths.** Click on the Trace Bitmap Icon to begin this process. As always, work from the top down through the dialog box. Select Black/White under Type of Tracing to Use. There are only two colors in our image, black and white, but with color images you can select how many colors to use and which ones to trace. Corner Fit allows you to soften sharp corners. Noise Filter can automatically remove small groups of pixels. This download does not have any pixels, but a scanned hand drawing may. Set Noise Filter to remove any random objects of 10 pixels or less. Finally, Bitmap Fading makes the image more transparent so you can see the trace results better. Check Group Vectors so the tracing becomes a single object to toolpath. Click on the Preview button at the bottom, and you will see black lines surrounding the entire carrot drawing. Note the gray color inside the lines; the image is still there under the tracing, but the default Bitmap Fading setting of 52% makes it appear gray. Click on the Apply button to accept the tracing, then exit the dialog box by clicking on Close. Select the image, leaving the trace deselected, and delete it to avoid confusion.

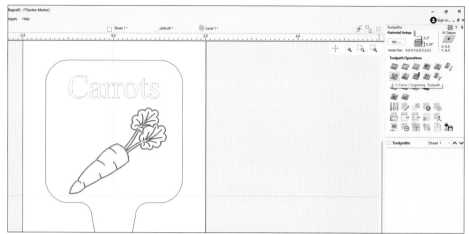

10 **Select the text and toolpath to begin carving and engraving.** The drawing, or CAD, phase of the project is complete, so click on the door icon to switch to the Toolpath commands on the right of the screen. The V-carving/engraving toolpath was used in Chapter 1 to ease you through your first run of the CNC, but now you can learn more about this toolpath. Select the text and click on the V-Carving/Engraving Toolpath icon to open the dialog box and get started.

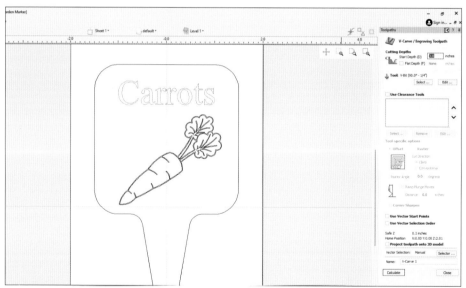

11 **Determine if you want to enter a cutting limit.** The first thing you should notice in the V-Carving/Engraving dialog box is that you do not enter a cutting depth. The depth of the cut is determined by the width of the letter or drawing area being carved and the angle of the engraving bit being used. You can set a start depth for the top of the stock (Z-axis 0.0) for this project, but if you wanted to carve inside a pocket like those in the tic-tac-toe game, you would enter the pocket depth here to start the engraving at the bottom of the pocket. Checking the small box lets you set a flat depth, which will limit the final depth of any wide areas being carved. You do not need a flat depth in this small project.

Engraving Angles Matter

You will notice that the V-Carving/Engraving Toolpath command does not require you to enter a cut depth like the profile and pocket toolpaths do. This is because the depth of the cut is determined by the width of the area being carved. The letters being carved in this project are outlines, and you are carving the space between.

The carving software automatically sets the cutting depth so the edges of the bit touch both sides of the carving. For example, if the letter is ⅛" (3mm) wide, and a 90-degree bit is being used, the depth of cut will be 1/16" (1.6mm). But a 60-degree V bit will cut 7/64" (2.7mm) deep in order to cut the full width of the letter. The depth of cut is constantly adjusted by the software to always fill the carving area, changing the depth of cut within a single letter or line as needed.

The size of your text and carvings will not change, but if your letters or carvings are small, selecting a bit with a sharper angle will result in deeper lines that will show up better and be less likely to be sanded out. If the area to be carved is wider than the bit, the software will program multiple cuts in steps downward to create a smooth angle to the bottom. Under the right conditions, this could mean cutting through the material. You always have the option of limiting the overall depth of cut. If you do, the bottom of the carving will be flat.

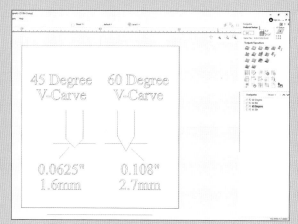

Try V bits with different angles for engraving. It can make a difference, especially with fine lines.

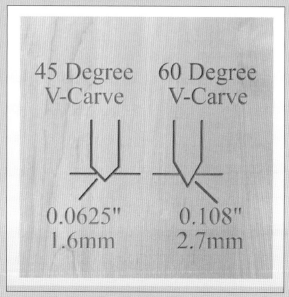

The width of the letters does not change, but the sharper V bit angle will cut them deeper into the stock.

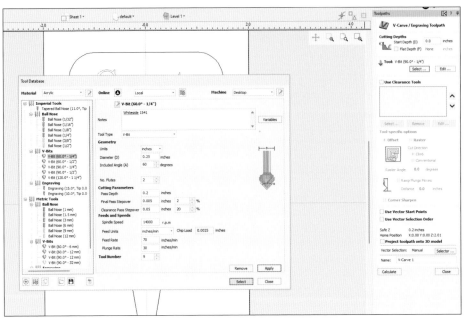

12 **Choose an engraving tool for your text.** Click the Select button to choose the tool for engraving your text, then load the 60-degree V bit. If your Tool Database does not have one loaded yet, you can change the angle of a 45-degree bit and resave it, keeping the same feeds and speeds. The rest of the data boxes are not used for this project, so just save the toolpath with whatever name you want.

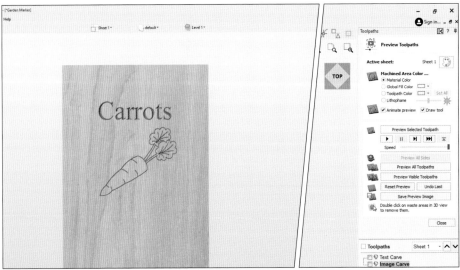

13 **Create the toolpath for the images.** Create the VCarve toolpath for the image using the same parameters—no depth setting, a 60-degree bit, no clearance tool—so just save it with a file name that will distinguish it from the text. Previewing the toolpaths clearly shows how the text and images will be carved into the workpiece. You could program the text and image cuts as a single toolpath, but it may not work as well if you choose different text or images later. Keeping them separate makes it easier to adapt this program for other designs.

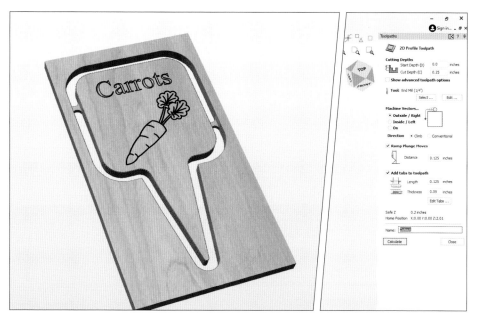

14 **Finish by programming the cutout of the tag.** This is a simple profile toolpath just like those in Chapters 2 and 3. Working down from the top, enter 0.25" (6mm) for the cut depth and select a straight bit for cutting out. Note: A ¼" (6mm) bit is being used here, but a ⅛" (3mm) would work just as well. Select Outside/Right for the Machine Vectors because you are keeping the part inside the lines. Set up the Ramp Plunge Moves and place a pair of staggered tabs on the sides as shown in the image above to keep the completed part from coming loose as it is cut out. Enter a file name for the toolpath, then click Calculate to finish the programming.

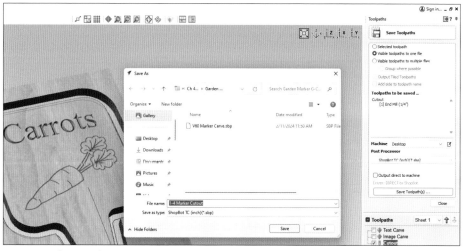

15 **Save the G-codes.** You need two G-codes because you are using two different router bits. Save the V bit G-code by selecting the two carving toolpaths and clicking on the Save Toolpath icon. Save the cutout toolpath as its own G-code. The names shown in the image above will work with machines that use a PC controller as well as those with a pendant, but name files in whatever way works for you.

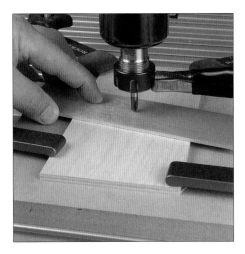

16 **Set up the CNC machine and start the run.** Turn your CNC on, home it, and get it ready to run according to your instruction manual, as you've done with the previous projects. Secure a 60-degree V bit into the chuck. Clamp your stock, with a backer underneath it, to the machine bed, then jog the head until the bit is pointing at the center of your plywood panel. Set the origin point to X-zero, Y-zero. Next, zero the Z-axis to the top of the stock either manually or with a touch plate if your machine has one. Call up the V bit G-code program and start the run. The machine will engrave the letters and the image, but do not be surprised if it skips around; this is normal.

Find and Fix Orphans

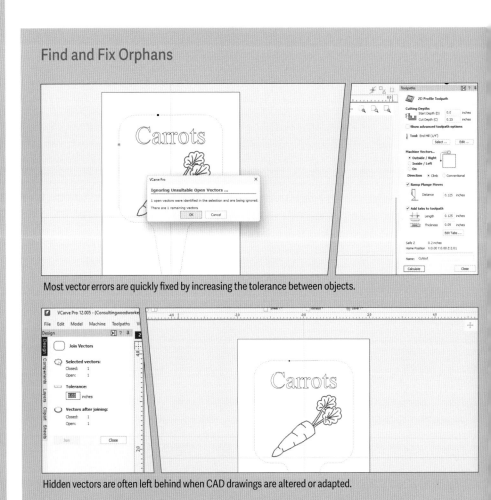

Most vector errors are quickly fixed by increasing the tolerance between objects.

Hidden vectors are often left behind when CAD drawings are altered or adapted.

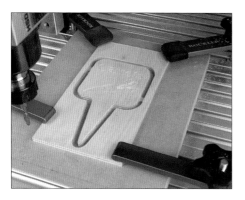

17 Finish the workpiece. Just as with the tic-tac-toe board in Chapter 3, you must reset the Z origin when changing bits. Mount the straight bit from your program into the router collet and set the Z height using that bit. Do not change the X or Y origin points; both G-code programs use the same start point. When the cutout is completed, unclamp the plywood from the bed, trim the tabs off, and lightly sand the edges. You can highlight the carvings with pencil or pen, then seal the garden marker with shellac or polyurethane. A spray can is excellent for this.

The techniques used in this project are readily adapted to create all sorts of signs, plaques, and engravings. You do not even have to make blanks and cut parts out. Serving trays, cutting boards, trophies, and many types of premade products can be customized with carved text and/or images.

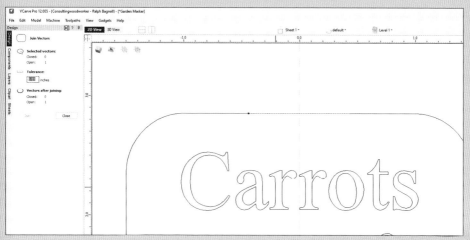

Learning to find orphans is more useful the more complex a project is.

When you import vectors created in other programs, you may have trouble applying toolpaths. Everything looks good, but when you try to calculate, you get an error message that looks something like the first picture on the left.

This error informs you that there is an extra line segment or arc hidden somewhere within the selected items. When the marker vectors were imported and joined, this **orphan** would have been indicated by the single open vector shown under Vectors after joining. Orphans can be hard to find, especially in more complex drawings, but there is a way to isolate them.

Working within the Join Vectors dialog box, click and drag the cursor over sections of the drawing and look at the results. If you select the lower section of the marker outline, you may see no open vectors, meaning that there are no orphans there, but when selecting the top half, an open vector shows up. Depending on your software, it may or may not be highlighted or have some sort of marker at the end(s) of the vector. By selecting smaller and smaller areas, you can isolate and delete the orphan.

CHAPTER 5

3D COASTER

Making relief carvings with your CNC provides you with a huge range of decorative elements for signs, plaques, boxes, and all sorts of projects. Creating the 3D models to carve is well beyond the scope of this book and requires a different level of software. But you have everything you need to import and carve an existing 3D model, and in this chapter you will. This coaster design features a basket-weave pattern carved into the bottom, making for an unusual and attractive design. You can make as many as you need for coaster sets to give as gifts or sell.

Supplies

- 5" (130mm) x 10" (250mm) x ⅜" (9.5mm) cherry or other closed-grain hardwood
- ¹⁄₁₆" (2mm) tapered ball nose bit (Freud 72-400 or similar)
- ¼" (6mm) straight bit (Whiteside RD 2076A or similar)

Skill Building

In this project, you will:
- Import a 3D .stl file.
- Orient, position, and scale a 3D model into the workspace.
- Create an outline for cutting the part out.
- Use the 3D finishing toolpath to program a relief carving.
- Reset the origin points to cut multiple parts from larger stock.

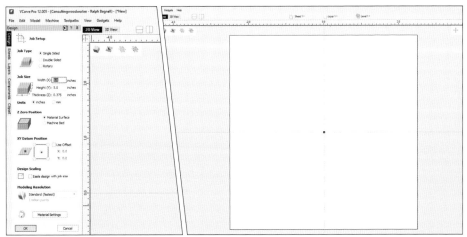

1 **Set up the job.** The coasters will be 3½" (89mm) square, and it is a good idea to include room for the clamps, so start a new job and set the size to 5" (125mm) in X and Y. Set the material thickness to ⅜" (9.5mm), the Z-zero to the top of the stock, and the XY datum position to be the center point. This is a new file, so there is no offset. Click the OK button at the bottom to close the dialog box.

These coasters make great gifts while introducing you to working with 3D models.

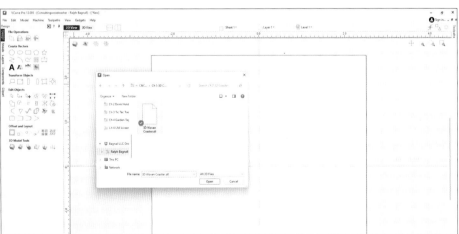

Download the companion files for this project by scanning the QR code above or visiting *www.foxpatterns.com/cnc-woodworking-for-the-absolute-beginner.*

2 Import the 3D model. You imported vectors in Chapter 2 and a bitmap (image) in Chapter 4. Now you will be importing an object. In the drop-down menu under File at the top left of the screen, select Import, then select Import Component/3D Model. There may also be an icon for importing models. From the files you downloaded for this book (available via the QR code above), select the .stl file labeled 3D Woven Coaster. When you click the Open button, the model will appear in VCarve as an entirely new screen you have not seen yet.

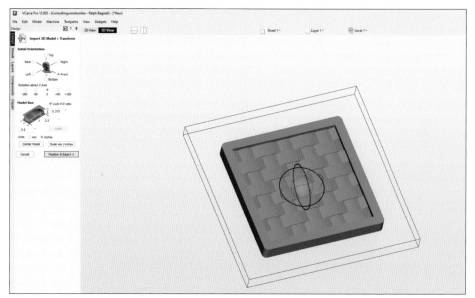

3 Orient the model. This page opens in a 3D **isometric** view, so you can choose how the model will be oriented and placed within your workpiece. Typically, dialog boxes are used to help with this. In VCarve, the Initial Orientation box provides a 3D image of a head with buttons that let you choose which point of view to work from. Models may import in odd positions, depending on how they were created. The Z-axis should read 0.375" (9.5mm) for this model. Choosing different circles around the icon in the Initial Orientation box will change the way the model sits within the X, Y, and Z axes. Scale the 3D model next. The imported .stl file will be in metric, so convert it if needed. In VCarve, use the Scale mm/inches button to do this. The coaster model imports at the right size, with the Z-axis set to 0.375" (9.5mm), so you will not need to change the scale. Click on the Center Model button to place the model in the middle of your virtual workpiece.

Bas Relief or "2 ½ D" Carving

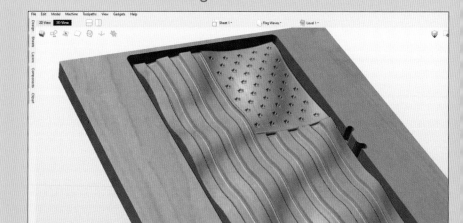

This flag carving was created by the author for *Woodworker's Journal Magazine* and Amana tools.

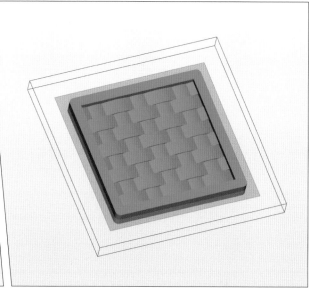

4 **Position and import the 3D model.** Click on the Position & Import button to open the next screen. The model will usually default to the middle of your stock. The coaster model was created to be the same ⅜" (9.5mm) thickness as the Job Setup, so it should already be centered. You can check by viewing the model from the X- or Y-axis view. Select one of these in the upper right corner of your screen, and the model should be within the stock lines. When it is set the way you want, click the Import button to finish the import and return to the virtual workspace. In VCarve, the 3D work is done within the Modeling tab, which you can see at the far left of the screen.

This chapter uses the term "3D carving" because that is what folks tend to say, but in fact the vast majority of CNC machines are not capable of carving in all three dimensions without specialized equipment and software. Fully carving a typical chess piece, for example, is simply not possible without rotating the part or the bit around the central axis as it is carved. What you are carving in this chapter is better known as "bas relief" carving, where shallow shapes are carved into a mostly flat surface. Unlike hand carving, the CNC cannot undercut any details, like the underside of a leaf, to give it dimension. Many programs allow for applying the carving onto a contoured surface, as shown in the flag carving that the author created for *Woodworker's Journal Magazine*, but that is about as "3D" as these machines can get without a fourth axis being added.

Changing the Scale

The scale can be changed by entering a new dimension in the X-, Y-, or Z-axis boxes provided. Keep the XYZ ratios locked so the model scales in all dimensions.

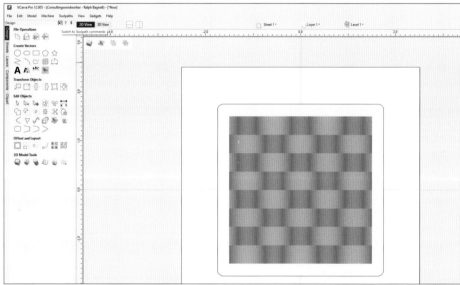

5 **Add a boundary around the model.** The 3D woven coaster will be shown within the virtual workspace. At the bottom of the icon window on the left, you will see some 3D icons. You'll want to cut the coaster out after carving, and most CAD/CAM programs have an option to automatically trace the boundary of your model, which you can toolpath later. The Create Vector Boundary around Selected Components icon on the left does this in VCarve. Click on 2D View at the top to return to the standard 2D virtual workspace. The view of the 3D model in 2D is interesting. The actual 3D parts are displayed in grayscale, where darker is deeper, lighter is shallower, and white is uncut. This is not just a visual reference; this is how the software sees the model and will cut the shapes. It converts photos for engraving the same way. Note also that there is now a vector showing the outer edges of the coaster. Your model is now ready to toolpath, so click on Toolpaths to switch to the Toolpath commands.

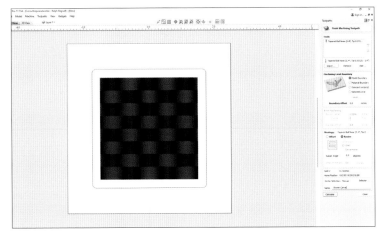

6 **Program the 3D toolpath.** Select the grayscale 3D model on the screen, then click on the 3D Finishing Toolpath to open the dialog box. Programming a 3D toolpath is surprisingly easy; it is similar to a pocket toolpath but with variable Z-axis cut depths taken from the model. There are not many choices to make. Choose the bit first. Select the tapered ball nose bit from the Tool Database. You can select a simple ball nose bit instead, as long as the tip radius is the same as your actual bit. The smaller radius creates finer carvings but takes longer to cut. Select Model Boundary to carve all the details, including the inside edges of the coaster pocket. Choose Raster Strategy for carving with the angle set to 0.0 degrees. This will align the cut direction with the grain to create the smoothest finish. Name to toolpath and click Calculate.

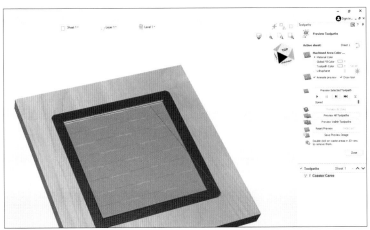

7 **Review the model before cutting.** The preview is where you will really see if everything is set up properly and confirm that the model will be cut at the proper depth. This view shows a good setup ready to save as a G-code. The toolpath lines actually start and end at the outer edges of the coaster with the Z-depth at 0 except within the pocket. The overlap makes sure that the edges of the pocket are cut as sharply as possible. Cutting out the coaster is similar to the cutting out the other projects, with the addition of a lead-in and a lead-out. You may have noticed that bits tend to leave tool marks where the cuts start and stop. This is because all bits flex a little when cutting. They flex throughout the cut in different ways as the bit moves into or out of the stock. Using leads, or a lead-in and a lead-out, starts and ends the cut away from the part, so any marks are left in the waste material. You get cleaner cuts that need less finish sanding.

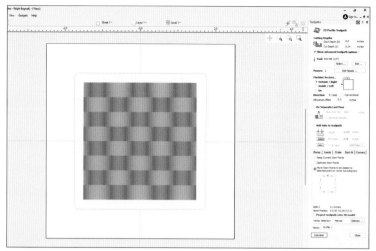

8 **Start programming the cutout.** Begin programming the cutout by clicking on the Profile Toolpath icon. Enter a cutting depth of 0.34" (8mm) to create an onion skin like in Chapter 3 and select a ¼" (6mm) straight bit for the cut. The option for leads may be visible in your CAD/CAM program. In VCarve, leads are among the few hidden options that only appear when you choose Show Advanced Toolpath Options where you set the cut depth. This expands the dialog box and offers four new options alongside Ramp: Leads, Order, Start At, and Corners. Click Start At first to choose the start point of the cut rather than use the default. You can choose any corner or side for the cut to start. Select the top, then click on Leads.

Specialty Carving Bits

Tapered ball nose carving bits are a relatively new item available to the CNC user.

Just as with V-carving and engraving, you can change the details and the look of your 3D carvings by choosing different bits. A common ball nose or core box bit can do some carving and is often the choice for the roughing cuts because the tip is usually ³⁄₁₆" (5mm) or larger. The smaller the tip, the finer the details that can be carved, so tapered ball nose bits (sometimes called pencil point or carving bits) were developed. These bits typically have a ¼" (6mm) shank with three or four cutting edges that taper to a small, round tip. The tips can be ½²" (0.8mm) up to ⅛" (3mm) in radius and have different taper angles. They are on the more expensive side, but they cut very clean and are durable enough to use for a long time. It is worth having one in your tool kit.

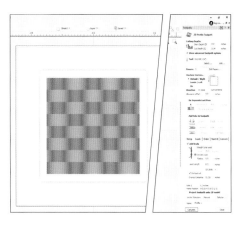

9 Program the leads. Leads are one of the tricks you can use to minimize the cleanup after a project is cut. Click Add Leads to activate the selections, then choose Circular Lead. You can experiment with all the options here and check the results in the Toolpath Preview. With the ¼" (6mm) bit being used for the cutout, 0.5" (12mm) works well for both the radius and the lead length. Select Do a Lead-Out and add in 0.125" (3mm) Overcut Distance to finish the leads. And add in a ramp with the leads. Type in the toolpath name and click Calculate to see the results.

10 Finish programming and begin the run. Save the tool paths as G-code files as you've done in the previous projects: one for the tapered ball nose bit and the other for the straight bit. Your 3D carving programs are complete and ready to run. Ready your CNC machine and clamp your stock in place. Note that the size of the stock called out at the beginning of this chapter is 5" (130mm) x 10" (250mm), not the 5" (130mm) x 5" (130mm) set up in the job size. This allows for cutting multiple parts from one oversized piece of stock. You could simply program two coasters side by side and cut them both at once, but that can be limiting. One part at a time can be cut from larger stock and has the advantage of being able to place each coaster where you want. The stock can't be smaller than the project, but it can always be larger. Cutting one at a time also lets you use leftover scraps of odd sizes and shapes or shift where you cut the coasters to avoid knots or other flaws in natural wood. For this project, you will cut two coasters from the stock but with only one tool change.

11 Secure the ball nose bit into the collet of your router. Then manually jog the head to the center of your first coaster, making sure you have at least 2 ½" (65mm) on each side clear for cutting. Set the X and Y origins to zero and touch off the bit to the top of the stock to set the Z height. Load the ball nose bit G-code you created and run the program.

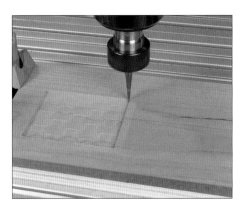

12 Begin carving the first coaster. The carving is revealed one line at a time as the bit cuts back and forth. The process is not quick, but it can create details that are a lot sharper than expected. Depending on your feed rate, it takes about twenty minutes to carve one of the coasters. As the run begins, you will see the bit tracing over the top of the stock but not cutting much because the rim of the coaster was part of the 3D model. This is normal and ensures a clean division between the rim and the carved bottom. When this carving is complete, do not switch to the straight bit to cut it out. Return the head to the start point, then manually jog into the uncut portion of the stock by 4½" (115mm) and reset the X, Y origin but not the Z-zero.

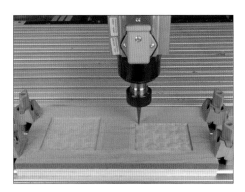

13 Carve the second coaster. A good distance for this project is 4½" (115mm). The move should always be more than the part size plus the cutout kerf widths with a bit extra added for safety. So 3½" (90mm) + ¼" (6mm) + ¼" (6mm) + ½" (13mm) = 4½" (115mm). You want a round number to make the jog easy to repeat. Load and run the same carving G-code again. When this carving is finished, switch to the straight bit, zero it to the surface of the stock, and then return to the X, Y origin.

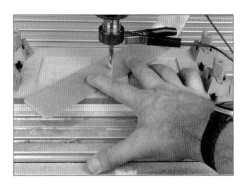

14 Finish the cutouts. Load the cutout G-code and run it from the current origin. Most CNC controllers have a button that returns the bit to whichever origin point is currently active. It makes this sort of cutting easier. When the cutout program finishes, return once more to the origin, then jog the head -4 ½" (-115mm) back over the first carving you made. Reset the X, Y origin to zero at this location and run the cutout G-code again. Two parts cut out with only one tool change! Of course, you can also set an origin and cut both G-codes before moving to the next coaster. It is good to have both options in your pocket.

There are many sources of 3D models that you can buy or even download for free, and now you know how to import them and mill them on your machine.

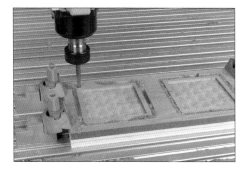

15 **Remove the stock from the machine after all the cutting is complete.** Separate the coasters from the waste and clean up the edges.

Experimenting with Models

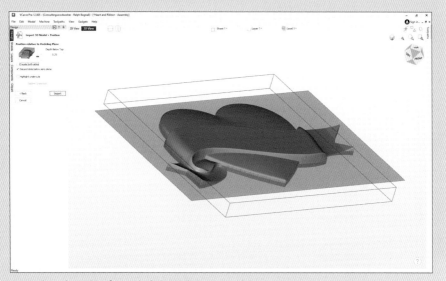

Learn about the options for manipulating 3D imports to widen your experience.

The 3D coaster model included in the download for this book (page 75) was created specifically to work with this chapter. You may find that other 3D models you want to import need to be oriented and positioned very differently and that can be challenging. But there are tools in the software to help.

To begin with, the model may be thinner or thicker than your stock. Experimenting with where you set the depth of the model can provide solutions. If the model is thicker than your stock, most programs allow for ignoring anything below the stock thickness solving the problem.

The heart and ribbon model here is a sample from Vectric that is ⅜" (9.5mm) thick. It can be set so the high point is right at the top of the stock, a little bit below, or even carved into the bottom of a deeper pocket. Adjusting model depths allows you to make them deeper or shallower within reason.

The model can be scaled to make it bigger or smaller, and if you unlock the three axes it can be stretched and distorted to create unique designs.

Your CNC can only carve details straight down from the top, with no undercuts. So a model of a car, for example, may need to be programmed as two parts such as top and bottom or left and right sides. This can be done with a combination of changing the orientation and ignoring the parts below the stock.

Experimenting with the settings and checking your results using the Preview Toolpath features in your software will quickly help you figure out what is really possible with your CNC Machine.

Glossary

This glossary is not meant to be regarded as an official list of definitions. Use this glossary as a reference when reading to understand unfamiliar terms as you encounter them.

A

Allowance: A predetermined amount by which the toolpath can be automatically offset from any raster line. This is useful for inlays and for making minor adjustments to holes and pockets without needing to redraw the part.

Array: A series of identical drawing items that are arranged in columns, rows, or circles in mechanical drawing.

B

Bit: The cutting tool mounted in the router or spindle of the CNC machine. This may be specially manufactured for use in CNC machines but does not need to be. Almost any common router bit that is not bearing-guided can be used in a CNC. See also Tool.

Bridge: The component of the CNC that moves forward and back along the frame of the machine. It holds the head, which moves side to side across the bridge. The front-to-back and the side-to-side motions make up the X- and Y-axes (which may vary between machines).

C

CAD: Computer-aided design; a computer program that allows the user to create drawings in scale with dimensions.

CAD/CAM: A computer program that combines drawing functions with toolpath functions, giving

users the capability to program CNC machines in one software package.

CAM: Computer-aided manufacturing; a computer program that associates or assigns physical milling operations to individual details contained within a vector drawing.

Cartesian coordinates: A system of locating objects within a field by defining points across a plane. Starting from a point chosen to be zero, all positions can be plotted by moving known distances in known directions.

Closed vector: A drawn object comprised of joined vector lines and arcs that form a single defined area with no gaps or overlaps between the ends of the segments. This prompts the CAD/CAM software to treat them as a single entity for cutting or pocketing inside or outside the shape.

CNC: Computer numerical control; referring to the guiding of machine processes and movement using software programs. The term has come to mean the machines themselves even more than the method of control.

Collet: A clamping piece used to hold router bits within the spindle or router motor.

D

Datum: The anchor point of a CAD drawing or CNC program. It is defined as 0 in all three axes, and all items in a drawing or movements in a

program relate to it. See also Start point.

DXF File: A file format that allows designs from different CAD programs to be easily and accurately shared within CAD/CAM programs.

E

End mill: A rotary cutting tool used in CNC machines. The term "end mill" is usually associated with metalworking, rather than woodworking, tools but most CNC router bits can be considered end mills.

F

Feed rate/feed speed: The speed at which the router bit moves across the part as it is cutting. This is usually stated in "inches per minute" or "mm per second." It is different than the RPM at which the bit is spinning at. See also RPM.

Fillet: A radius added to a square corner or edge.

Flat depth: A command that allows for limiting the depth of the carving, preventing it from cutting deeper than desired. When carving with a V bit, the depth of cut is variable, defined by the bit meeting both sides of the vector being cut.

Form tool: A form tool is usually what you would consider a profile router bit. The tool database already has categories for standard bits, but you can add profiles like round overs and goes under the form tool category so you can see the profile you draw in the 3D preview.

G

G-code: A text file created from the CAD/CAM software that actually runs the CNC machine. This is a universal set of instructions that can be adapted to nearly any model of machine.

Going home: A button command on a controller to automatically return the machine head to the current zero or start point.

H

Hard home: A mechanical origin point that cannot be changed; all operations on the CNC machine are computed from this point. It differs from other home positions because it cannot be easily changed, if at all. See also Home.

Head: The part that holds the router or spindle to which the tool is attached. This section can move in the X-, Y-, and Z-axes.

Home: The mechanical origin of the machine itself, preset origin points that can be selected, or a predetermined start point for a particular program. See also Hard home.

Homing: An automated process that the machine may need to execute upon system start-up to physically find the mechanical origin point.

I

Interpolate: To mill a hole to diameter using a bit that is smaller than the hole. This improves bit life by reducing overheating and allows for easy adjustment of the size of the hole being milled.

Isometric: A drawing or 3D model seen in side or top view may not always show a true version of the object. An isometric view allows an object to be viewed in an angled view which shows a side and face combined for better understanding.

J

Jog: To move the head by pressing a button and moving it manually or by entering a set distance for the head to move on command.

L

Lead-in/lead-out: Setting the tool path to start and end beyond the part outline for cleaner edges. All machines and bits flex somewhat under load, and using a lead-in/lead-out avoids this flex showing up as a tool mark on the part that will need to be sanded off later.

M

Machine bed: The Z-axis start point of a CAD/CAM program when working from the machine bed upward. See also Material surface.

Material surface: The Z-Axis start point of a CAD/CAM program when working from the top of the workpiece. See also Machine bed.

MDF: Medium density fiberboard; this is an inexpensive man-made sheet product made by grinding wood into pulp and then pressing it into flat panels with a binding agent. MDF is easy to mill and dimensionally more consistent than plywood.

O

Onion skin: A thin layer of material left behind by intentionally cutting too shallow. This is an effective method of holding parts as they are cut out. The onion skin can be quickly sanded off after milling. See also Tabs.

Open vector: Vector lines and arcs that are not connected end-to-end to enclose a given space. Open vectors have no inside or outside, so they cannot be used for pockets or cutting out parts. See also Closed vectors.

Orphan: Hidden line segments, arcs, and circles are referred to as orphans. In complex drawings, they can be very challenging to locate and delete. They can be accidentally created when creating or editing drawings.

P

Post processor: A translation program that takes the data within the CAD/CAM program and rewrites it into a G-code file that is tailored to a specific type of CNC machine.

Plug: Uncut waste material left inside a toolpath when holes or other openings are cut within a part.

Preview function: A 3D computer model of the proposed toolpaths provided by CAD/CAM programs. This is highly useful for checking your programs before cutting stock.

R

Raster: An art file, such as a bitmap or JPEG, made up of pixels. Rasters cannot be read or used in programming CNC machines; they must be converted to vectors. See also Vectors.

Router: The motors from hand-held routers are often used to power the tools in an entry-level CNC machine as opposed to a dedicated spindle. See also Spindle.

RPM: Stands for revolutions per minute and defines how rapidly the router bit is spinning as it cuts. Higher-end benchtop CNC machines can control the RPM of the spindle, while others need the RPM to be set manually on the router before cutting. See also Spindle speed.

S

Saved home positions: Home positions that remain in the machine's memory, even through system start-up, until the operator resets them. See also Home.

Shank: The body of a router bit or end mill that is clamped into a collet when held in a router or spindle motor.

Single Line fonts: Fonts typically made from vector lines rather than from the outlines that True Type lines are made from. Single Line fonts are often used to create text by cutting directly on the lines. See also True Type fonts.

Spindle: A motor that is purpose-built for use on a CNC machine. It has a collet to hold bits and serves the same function as when a handheld router motor is used. See also Router.

Snap/snapping: To make drawing easier, the software assumes that you will want to start and end items you are drawing at the end points or centers of parts you have already drawn. So with snap mode on, as your cursor gets close to any of these points, it will jump or "snap" to the point.

Spindle speed: The rotational speed of the motor turning the router bit. A CNC with a spindle (rather than a router) can often control the spindle speed through the G-code. See also RPM.

Spoil board: A secondary surface added to the machine bed of a CNC that protects the bed when parts are cut all the way through.

Start point: The base location from which all features of a drawing or locations in a program are calculated. It is typically zero in the X-, Y-, and Z axes. See also Datum.

Step overs: Side-by-side passes of the bit over areas that need to be milled wider than the bit. These passes continue until the pocket is complete and are overlapped to ensure that all the stock is cut.

T

Tabs: Small uncut sections in the perimeter cut that hold the part in place and prevent it from getting caught in the bit and damaged or even thrown from the machine. Tabs are separated from the part after cutting is complete. See also Onion skin.

Temporary home position: A home position that can be set manually at any time but is not saved if the system is shut down or a different home is selected. See also Home.

Three-axis CNC: Most CNC machines move the bit in three directions, also called axis; Front to back, side to side, and up and down. These axes are referred to as X, Y, and Z.

Tool: Also Tooling. Another word for the router bit used in the CNC for cutting operations. Most CAD/CAM software programs use the term tool where most of us would say bit. See also Bit.

Tool database: Your Tool Database stores all the information for a single router bit so the software can automatically use it when calculating the toolpaths. This saves you from having to enter all this information every time you choose a bit.

Toolpath: The set of instructions that control how a cut is made, including the tool to use, the depth of cut, the feed rate, the tool offset, and similar information.

True Type font: A font in which the letters are made up of outlines rather than made up of single lines. True Type fonts work very well for V-carving. See also Single Line fonts.

V

Vector: Lines drawn between known points in a CAD drawing. Because all movement commands within a G-code program need specific X and Y coordinates, CAD/CAM programs require vectors for drawings rather than image files such as bitmaps or JPEGs. See also Rasters.

W

Workpiece: The material to be cut by the CNC, such as wood, plastic, and the like.

Work holding: The generic term for how stock is clamped to the machine during milling. It can be as simple as double-faced tape or as complex as vacuum hold-down fixtures.

Workspace: The virtual area in a CAD/CAM program where the drawing is created and/or toolpathed.

Z

Zero/origin/start point: A term that usually refers to the start point or origin of a program.

Index

Note: Page numbers in *italics* indicate projects. Page numbers in **bold** indicate glossary definitions.

About the Author

Industry leader and woodworking expert Ralph Bagnall has been working with CNC machines since the mid-1990s. He spent several years selling CNCs and other woodworking equipment, as well as installing machinery and training operators. The Founder of Consulting Woodworker, a company specializing in physical plant consulting, video production, and marketing services for the woodworking industry, Ralph also hosts *Woodcademy TV*, where he teaches tips, tricks, and techniques that woodworkers of all skill levels can apply in their shops. His written work has been published in national magazines, including *Woodworker's Journal*, *Woodcraft*, and *Woodshop News*. He is also a frequent speaker at prominent woodworking events, such as the International Woodworking Fair, National Wood Flooring Association Show, and The International Surfaces Exhibition. To learn more about Ralph, visit *www.Woodcademy.com* or *www.ConsultingWoodworker.com*.